ROADMAP™  B1

WORKBOOK
with key and online audio

Kate Browne, Claire Fitzgerald

CONTENTS

3

Vocabulary
Personal details

1 **Choose the correct alternatives.**

1 I'd like to *do*/*make* a degree one day.

2 I don't enjoy *taking*/*training* exams.

3 It would be nice to *do*/*run* my own company one day.

4 *Getting*/*Passing* qualifications is important if you want a good job.

5 I'm studying, but I also work *part*/*half* time.

6 My brother is training *as*/*like* a lawyer.

7 When I have time, I'd like to do a *course*/*lesson* in ancient history.

8 My sister is *passing*/*studying* for a degree right now.

2 **Decide if the sentences are correct (✓) or incorrect (✗). Then correct the incorrect sentences.**

1 My sister is doing a course economics.   ✗
   My sister is doing a course in economics.

2 I want to study for a qualification in business.

3 I have a degree English and French.

4 I hope that I pass my exams this year.

5 I'm training for tour guide with a local company.

6 I'm taking my final exams in May.

7 My mother runs her own company. She's always very busy!

8 I work part of time in my local supermarket at the weekends.

3 **Complete the text with the words in the box.**

as	for	in	pass	run	time

I'm studying ¹ *for* my degree in business at the moment and I'm really enjoying it. I really hope I ² _____ my exams at the end of the year! I don't know what I want to do yet when I finish. I'm working ³ _____ time at a local restaurant to help pay for my studies, and maybe I'll do a course ⁴ _____ Spanish later this year, too. Then I could travel abroad for a while after my degree.

How about you? Are you still working ⁵ _____ a lawyer? I know you said you'd like to ⁶ _____ your own company one day. Have you decided which area you'd like to work in?

Grammar
Present simple and present continuous

4 **Complete the conversations with the present simple or continuous form of the verbs in brackets.**

1 A: What _____*do*_____ you _____*do*_____ (do)?
   B: I _____ (be) a teacher. I work full-time in a local school.

2 A: We like to get up early. We usually _____ (wake) up at five in the morning and get to work by eight.
   B: Me too! I _____ (not get) up at five though! That's too early for me!

3 A: My father _____ (have got) a really big family – five brothers and four sisters!
   B: Wow! That's huge! I _____ (be) an only child.

4 A: James _____ (take) an art course this year and he finds it really interesting.
   B: That's great. I really _____ (want) to do something like that. Maybe I can join, too!

5 A: I love reading in my spare time. Actually, I _____ (read) a really good novel at the moment. It's called *The Dark*.
   B: Oh, I read that last year. I _____ (think) it's awful!

6 A: How often _____ Jane _____ (go) to the gym?
   B: Hm, she usually _____ (go) every evening, except at the weekends. She takes the weekends off!

7 A: How _____ the new course _____ (go), John?
   B: It's difficult. I _____ (train) to be a nurse and the hours are really long.

8 A: Hurry up, Julie! We _____ (leave) now!
   B: Wait! I _____ (come)!

5 **There is one missing word in items 1–7. Write an ✗ where the word is missing. Then write the missing word at the end of each sentence.**

1 I love my life here. I ✗ living in the centre and working full time in an office. It's great!   *am*

2 Why you studying English? _____

3 They taking a course in creative writing. It sounds really interesting. _____

4 I never see Sara these days. She studying for a qualification in marketing and she is working really hard. _____

5 What they looking at? _____

6 Don't use your phone! You driving! _____

7 Sorry, but we can't go to the party. We are really busy this month as we working on an important project. _____

8 He not speaking to her at the moment. They had an argument. _____

Vocabulary
Personal characteristics

1 Complete the missing words.

1 Beth is so r _eliabl_e. When she says she'll do something, she'll do it!

2 My sister is so kind and c_____g. She always helps other people.

3 I'm going to ask Laura for advice. She always tells the truth. She's really h_____t.

4 As a teacher, you need to be p_____t. Some people learn more slowly than others and can be quite s_____e when you correct them.

5 I'm seeing Paul tomorrow and I hope he's finished his part of the project. He can be so l_____y sometimes!

6 I get really nervous when I have to speak in front of people. I'm so s_____y. I wish I was more c_____t!

7 You have to be a_____s and h_____d-w_____g to do well at work. You should set clear goals and think about how you're going to reach them.

8 Running your own company means that you need to be o_____d. There's a lot to do and not a lot of time to do it.

9 One of the hardest things about being a writer is being c_____e. It isn't always easy to think of new ideas.

2 Use the clues to complete the crossword.

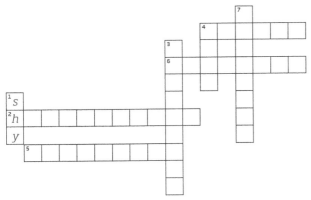

Across

2 If you do a lot of work, you are a _____ person. (11)

4 If you like helping people, you are a _____ person. (6)

5 If you want to do well at work, you are _____ (9)

6 If people trust you, you are a _____ person. (8)

Down

1 If you get nervous when meeting new people, you are _____ (3)

3 If you plan what to do every day, you are an _____ person. (9)

4 If you are relaxed and don't worry about things, you are a _____ person. (4)

7 If you love performing, painting or drawing, you are _____ (8)

Grammar
be going to and present continuous

3 Complete the conversation with one word in each gap.

A: We ¹ ___'re___ leaving to meet Sarah and Mike for lunch in about ten minutes. Why don't you come along?

B: I can't. I ² _____ meeting my manager at one.

A: Really! That sounds serious! What about?

B: Well, we're ³ _____ to talk about my future in the company.

A: Oh! What ⁴ _____ you going to say?

B: I'm going ⁵ _____ ask about training to become a project manager. I'm quite nervous about it, actually!

A: Don't be! Everybody knows that you do an amazing job.

B: Hm, I hope you're right! Hey, some friends ⁶ _____ coming for dinner on Saturday. Do you want to come?

A: Sure, sounds good. Good luck with the meeting!

4a Put the words in the correct order to make questions.

1 What / to do after university / is she / going / ?
   What is she going to do after university?

2 are we / seeing / this week / When / Tim / ?
   _____

3 going / you leave school / What / to do / when / are you / ?
   _____

4 What / course / on Tuesday / are you / starting / ?
   _____

5 are they / staying / next weekend / How long / ?
   _____

6 is David / going / in the future / to do / What / ?
   _____

b Match questions 1–6 in Exercise 4a with responses a–f.

a From Saturday afternoon until Sunday evening. ___5___

b He doesn't know. He's thinking about it. _____

c French, but it's actually not starting until Wednesday. _____

d I'm going to study for a degree in engineering. _____

e We're meeting him on Friday night. _____

f She's going to travel abroad for a year. _____

1c

Vocabulary
Describing change

1 Choose the correct alternatives.

1 The number of cars on the road is *going up/going down*. Everyone's really happy about it.

2 We've got some great people here. I'm sure the situation will *improve/get worse*.

3 It's becoming *easier/harder* for young people to find a well-paid job these days. Because of this, many of them are staying at home with their parents instead of renting apartments.

4 Crime is *rising/falling* in the area because there are more police on the streets.

5 More and more people are moving to cities, so the population of small towns and villages is *decreasing/increasing*.

6 The number of accidents is *rising/going down*, and many people are asking what we can do to change the situation.

2 Complete the second sentence so that it means the same as the first.

1 The number of people without jobs is increasing.
The number of people without jobs is r *ising* .

2 I hope the situation gets better.
I hope the situation i_____ .

3 There aren't so many tourists coming these days.
The number of tourists is f_____ .

4 It's becoming more difficult to find a house these days.
It's g_____ h_____ to find a house these days.

5 Because of the new rules, it won't be so difficult to get a visa.
Getting a visa is g_____ e_____ .

6 The number of visitors went up in January.
The number of visitors i_____ in January.

7 There won't be so many students in the class this year.
The number of students will g_____ d_____ this year.

8 There won't be so much work next year.
The amount of work will d_____ next year.

Grammar
will for prediction

3 Choose the correct alternatives.

> **The future of the classroom**
>
> In the future, the way we learn languages ¹*will/does* change. Technology ²*will to/will* get better and this will ³*helping/help* to make lessons more interesting and interactive. The use of digital tools such as tablets will ⁴*increases/increase* and fewer people will ⁵*use/using* textbooks.
>
> Experts predict that the 'online classroom' will become more popular and students ⁶*will/are* have lessons at home, which means that people won't ⁷*have/having* to travel very far to school. Some people even say that robots will ⁸*to replace/replace* people as teachers! Whatever happens, the classrooms of the future will certainly be different!

4 Complete the sentences with *will* or *won't* and the verbs in brackets.

1 I don't believe the population of our country ___*will fall*___ (fall) in ten years' time.

2 She _____ (not go) to university next year if she gets poor exam results.

3 Do you think it _____ (be) sunny tomorrow? Yes, I think so!

4 I'm certain he _____ (pass) his exams at the end of the year. He works so hard.

5 We hope that everybody _____ (have) jobs in the future.

6 Scientists are sure that temperatures _____ (rise) and the planet will become hotter in a few years' time.

7 Robots _____ (not replace) teachers. I'm sure of it!

8 _____ the weather _____ (get worse)? Yes, it will.

5 Complete the sentences with *will* or *won't* and the words and phrases in the box.

> probably arrive late   be angry with   carry money
> ~~come to the party~~   go on holiday   stay here

1 He's pretty lazy. I don't think he ___*will come to the party*___ tonight.

2 He didn't do his homework, so the teacher _____ him.

3 She's not happy in the job. She _____ long.

4 We _____ in the future. We'll pay for everything by card.

5 If she comes to the meeting, she _____ . I hate it when she does that.

6 I don't think we _____ . We don't have the money.

Functional language

Make and respond to suggestions

1 Choose the correct response to complete the conversations.

1 I'm so bored at the moment. I have nothing to do at the weekends!
   a <u>How about taking up a hobby?</u>
   b How about take up a hobby?

2 I really need to improve my English vocabulary. I always use the same words.
   a I recommend to read in English.
   b I recommend reading in English.

3 Jim is training to be an outdoor instructor at the moment.
   a Really? That sound interesting.
   b Really? That sounds interesting.

4 I'm so stressed at the moment. I'm working really hard.
   a Why not try running? It's a great way to reduce stress.
   b Why not to try run? It's a great way to reduce stress.

5 Why isn't Nina coming to the cinema with us this evening?
   a Oh, she's not keen in the cinema. She prefers watching films at home.
   b Oh, she's not keen on the cinema. She prefers watching films at home.

6 Oh no! It's going to rain all day on Saturday!
   a Well, I don't fancy to hike then. Let's do something else.
   b Well, I don't fancy hiking then. Let's do something else.

2 Choose the correct alternatives.

1 I'm not *sure/keen* camping is a good idea – the weather isn't very good at the moment. Let's book a hotel instead.

2 Why *don't/not* try doing something different in the evenings, like going to an art or music class?

3 You're planning a surprise party? That *sounds/sound* great! I'm sure Karen will love it!

4 If you're feeling tired I recommend *watch/watching* less TV and exercising more. You'll feel much better!

5 Spending time with friends is very good *for/to* your health – people who relax and socialise are usually happier and less stressed.

6 I'm not keen *about/on* running. I prefer playing team sports like football and rugby.

3 Complete the conversation with the phrases in the box.

> a brilliant idea   here's another idea   I think   not try running
> on doing sport   ~~sounds really interesting~~   taking up a hobby
> you to forget

A: Hi Mel! Congratulations on your new job! It ¹ *sounds really interesting* .

B: Thanks, Dave. I'm really happy, but it's stressful. I'm working a lot and feel really tired.

A: How about ² _____ ? I think it's really important to have time for yourself. Why ³ _____ ?

B: Hmm. I'm not keen ⁴ _____ . I hate getting dirty!

A: Well, ⁵ _____ . What about doing a course in art or creative writing? ⁶ _____ you'll enjoy it as you are so creative.

B: That's ⁷ _____ ! Thanks, Dave!

A: No problem. I did one last year and I loved it. It really helps ⁸ _____ about everything and relax.

Listening

1 🔊 1.01 **Listen to a radio programme about homeworking and choose the correct option a, b, or c.**

a They discuss the positive things about working from home.

b They discuss the negative things about working from home.

c They discuss the positive and negative things about working from home.

2 Listen again and choose the correct alternatives.

1 *Everyone/Not everyone* agrees that working from home is a good idea.

2 The presenter thinks it *is usually/isn't very* difficult these days for people to meet online.

3 Michael thinks it can be *useful/ a waste of time* talking to colleagues outside of meetings.

4 Michael thinks that working from home in winter is *good/bad* for the environment.

5 The presenter suggests we could work from home only *in the summer/ when it's cold outside*.

6 Some business owners prefer it when they can *see/phone* their employees.

7 Michael thinks that stress can have a *positive/negative* effect on how productive employees are.

8 The presenter *would/wouldn't* like to work from home.

3a Decide if the sentences are true (T) or false (F).

1 Michael thinks if people work at home, relationships will improve.   *F*

2 Michael thinks talking to colleagues helps people develop new ideas.   _____

3 The presenter wants fewer cars on the roads.   _____

4 If people work from home, we use less heating.   _____

5 All managers like the idea of homeworking.   _____

6 Happier and more motivated people are more productive.   _____

b Listen again and check your answers.

Reading

1 **Read the blog post. Who is it for? Choose the correct option a, b or c.**

a confident people who want to meet more friends

b people who want advice about talking to new people

c people who want to host parties in their home

2 **Read the blog post again and answer the questions.**

1 What do most people find difficult when they meet each other for the first time?

2 What advice does the writer give about questions to ask people?

3 Why is finding things in common a good idea?

4 Why shouldn't you say things which aren't true to make people feel good?

5 What two things does the writer say we should use to show interest?

6 Why is over-politeness not recommended?

3 **Complete the ideas from the blog post with one word.**

1 Ask _questions_ to find common ground.

2 You can tell someone the work they do is _____ .

3 Don't _____ too much. Let the other person speak!

4 Show that you're _____ in what the other person is saying.

5 If you are too polite, people might feel _____ .

4 **Find the words in bold below in the blog post and complete the definitions.**

1 A **tip** is *a piece of advice*/ *a problem*. (paragraph 1)

2 **Common ground** means having *similar*/ *different* interests. (paragraph 2)

3 A **compliment** is made to make someone feel *good*/ *bad*. (paragraph 3)

4 A **host** is the person who *receives guests in their home*/ *is invited* somewhere. (paragraph 3)

5 **Insincere** behaviour suggests you are being *honest*/ *dishonest*. (paragraph 3)

Topics   Podcasts   Downloads   About

MEETING PEOPLE

1 We've all felt some fear when we've been invited to a party or asked to talk at a work meeting or conference. Both social and professional events can be scary for the shy and even the most confident. But why? For most people, it's the social interaction in these situations. We have to make small talk and we have to find things in common with a complete stranger – this is not easy. Need some help? Read our tips below.

ICEBREAKERS

2 The first thing we need is some easy questions to ask. Keep it simple at first. For example, if you're at a party, you could ask: *How do you know the host?* If it's a work conference, you could ask: *Where do you work / What department are you in? Do you know … ?* Don't be afraid of asking personal questions – people like talking about themselves. Just make sure the questions aren't too personal! The idea is that you find some common ground to make conversation easier. As soon as you find things in common, you'll find that you suddenly have a lot of things to say to each other.

BE POSITIVE AND NICE

3 Most people like a compliment. Who doesn't like to be told that their job is interesting or that they tell funny jokes? If you're at a party and you don't know the host very well, start by admiring their home. You could say: *What wonderful views you have!* If it's a work event, maybe you've heard a talk by the person you're speaking to. In this case, you could be honest and say: *I heard you give a very interesting talk last year on …* This will lead to more conversation openers. However, don't be too nice. Give people compliments about things you really like about them. If you give a false compliment, they might notice and think you're insincere.

BE A GOOD LISTENER

4 Sometimes when we want to give a good impression we make the mistake of speaking too much; we think we have to impress our listener, so we tell our stories and share our experiences and forget to ask about the other person. Everyone likes sharing, so make sure you ask questions to find out about your new friend and more importantly, listen! To actively listen, use words and body language to show interest. My favourites are: *Really? Wow, how interesting!* and *Well, I never knew that!* This will make the conservation a positive experience for both of you. But, remember, don't be afraid of silence – it's a normal part of conversation.

BE YOURSELF

5 This is the most important thing to remember. Everybody likes honesty, so don't be afraid to make jokes and be yourself! Be respectful, but don't be too polite. Over-politeness can make people feel uncomfortable. You want to make both of you feel comfortable, so be open and relaxed!

Writing

1 Read the application and answer the questions.

1 What job is Ross applying for?

2 Why does Ross think he would be good for the job?

Dear Mrs Barranger,

I am writing regarding the senior accountant position currently advertised on your website. Please find attached a copy of my CV.

I have worked in the industry for over 11 years, and I also have an ACCA diploma in accounting. I have developed all the necessary skills for the role that you are offering in my present position as an accountant for Synatech. In my role at Synatech, I am responsible for managing two junior accountants, and I think this makes me a very strong candidate for your senior position. I like working in a team, and enjoy helping people to develop their skills.

I would love to discuss the role with you in person. If you would like to get in touch to discuss my application and to arrange an interview, you can contact me on this email address or by phone.

I look forward to hearing from you soon.

Yours sincerely,

Ross Gardley

2 Read the Focus box. Then read the sentences below and decide if they should be placed in the beginning of an application (B), the middle (M) or the end (E).

Using paragraphs in a job application

Pieces of writing are usually organised into paragraphs. Paragraphs make it easier for a reader to find the information they need. Each paragraph usually deals with a different part of the topic, so it's easy for a reader to know where they can find the information they need. Many job applications are organised in the following way:

First paragraph: This tells the reader why you are writing.

Middle paragraph(s): This is where you communicate the main information, what makes you a good candidate for the job, including details of education and work experience.

Final paragraph: This tells the reader what you hope/ want to happen next.

a I have worked with the same systems that you use at ITTX for several years.   _M_

b Dear Mr Laconti, ...

c I would love the opportunity to discuss the role face to face.   ....

d Please find my CV attached.   ....

e I also work with a similar-size team in my current position at Belsander, so I don't think it would be difficult for me to adapt to the new role.   ....

f You can contact me at any time at this email address or by phone.   ....

g I look forward to hearing from you.   ....

h I feel I am a strong candidate for the developer position.   ....

i I'm writing to express my interest in the developer position which I saw advertised online.   ....

j Steven Jones   ....

Prepare

3 You're going to apply for a job as a fitness instructor. Read the notes below and think about what else you can say.

- saw advert – Jungle gym
- ten years' experience as an instructor
- love helping people, patient and hard-working
- can start immediately

Write

4 Write your application email. Remember to put your writing into appropriate paragraphs. Use your notes in Exercise 3 and the email in Exercise 1 to help you.

Vocabulary

Describing feelings and events

1 Complete the sentences with the adjectives in the box.

annoyed   disappointed   embarrassed   frightened
relaxed   worried

1 Someone is talking loudly on their phone at work and you're trying to concentrate. You feel _____ .

2 You see someone who you know at a party, but you've forgotten their name. You feel _____ .

3 You're camping in a forest and hear a strange noise. You feel _____ .

4 You're lying on a sofa watching your favourite TV programme. You feel _____ .

5 You receive your exam results, but you've failed. You feel

_____ .

6 Your sister hasn't answered her phone for a week and you're trying to contact her. You feel _____ .

2 Choose the correct alternatives.

1 It's very *annoying/relaxing* when people shout.

2 Walking in the country is very *relaxing/worrying*.

3 I get *embarrassed/surprised* when I have to speak in public.

4 When I go somewhere new, I get *excited/disappointed* thinking about all the new things I'll see.

5 That horror film was *frightening/tiring*. I couldn't sleep all night!

6 The storm last week was *disappointing/surprising*. The weather forecast was completely wrong!

7 I didn't sleep very well last night, so I'm very *tired/embarrassed* today.

8 I was really excited about that film, but it was really *disappointing/relaxing*.

9 The price of petrol keeps going up. It's really *worrying/embarrassing*.

10 I met my ex-boyfriend in town yesterday, and he was with his new girlfriend. It was really *embarrassing/disappointing*.

3 Complete the adjectives with *-ing* or *-ed*.

1 I was *surpris_ed_* when I saw my exam results!

2 Travelling around the world was an *amaz____* experience.

3 Working late makes me feel very *tir____* .

4 Climate change is very *worry____* .

5 I love staying in and reading a good book – I find it very *relax____* .

6 She felt *embarrass____* when she fell over in the street.

7 I'm *excit____* about my trip.

8 It was raining very hard when I drove home – it was very *frighten____* .

Grammar

Past simple and past continuous

4 Choose the correct alternatives.

A: First caller, hello. What ¹*did you do/were you doing* when the Berlin Wall came down?

B: Well, it's difficult to believe, but I ²*was being/was* there in West Berlin and I saw all the celebrations. It was amazing.

A: ³*Did you see/Were you seeing* anything interesting?

B: Oh yes – when I got to the wall, everyone ⁴*was having/had* a great time and lots of people ⁵*were standing/stood* on the wall.

A: That sounds amazing. Caller two. Can you tell us about your experience?

B: Of course. I ⁶*learnt/was learning* German at the time, so I was in Berlin, and on that night I was in town with some German friends. No one could believe what ⁷*was happening/happened*. We were having a drink when suddenly everyone started shouting. I was frightened at first, but then I ⁸*heard/was hearing* someone say 'the wall is down'. We thought it was a joke, but when we saw the police, we realised it was true.

5 Use the prompts to write sentences with the past simple and past continuous.

1 Someone call / when / I give a class
   Someone called when I was giving a class.

2 She met husband / when / she study English at university

_____

3 I wait for a bus for one hour / when / three come at once!

_____

4 He travel / when / he meet an old friend

_____

5 My niece call / when / I watch TV

_____

6 I walk to the station / when / I realise / I (not) have my phone

_____

Vocabulary
Memories

1 Complete the sentences with the words in the box.

> forget   makes   memories   of
> reminds   think

1 The smell of cut grass _____ me of England.
2 The sound of church bells makes me _____ of my school days.
3 The song *Walk Away* _____ me happy.
4 The feel of clean sheets makes me think _____ my grandmother.
5 I'll never _____ the taste of my mother's lemon pie.
6 I have happy _____ of my grandparents' house.

2 Rewrite the sentences using the words in brackets so that they mean the same.

1 The smell of newly cut grass always reminds me of summer.
The smell of newly cut grass _____*makes me think of*_____ summer. (think)

2 The taste of paella makes me think of holidays in Spain.
The taste of paella _____ holidays in Spain. (reminds)

3 I feel happy when I hear birds singing.
The sound of birds singing _____ happy. (makes)

4 I'll always remember the day the Berlin Wall came down.
I'll _____ the day the Berlin Wall came down. (forget)

5 When I think of my school days, I feel happy.
I have _____ of my school days. (memories)

6 I'll never forget the day my sister got married.
I'll _____ the day my sister got married. (remember)

7 When I walk down this road, I remember walking to school when I was young.
Walking down this road _____ when I was young. (reminds)

8 I remember arriving in Rome. It was an amazing experience.
I _____ in Rome. (forget)

Grammar
used to

3 Correct the mistake in each sentence.

1 I didn't ~~used~~ ^*use* to go camping as a child.

2 I used to meeting my friends every Saturday.

3 She don't use to like her job, but she does now.

4 He didn't use get good marks at school.

5 I use to love the taste of roast chicken, but I can't stand it now!

6 Did you used to play sports when you were at school?

7 We used to smoked, but we quit a couple of years ago.

8 We are used to go on holidays to France every summer.

4 Write sentences about Mark using the information in brackets. Use *used to*.

1 *Mark used to be single, but now he's married.*
(past: be single, now: be married)

2 _____
(past: wear jeans a lot, now: wear a suit to work)

3 _____
(past: go to school, now: work in an office)

4 _____
(past: do a lot of exercise, now: not do any exercise)

5 _____
(past: not cook, now: love cooking)

6 _____
(past: ride a bicycle, now: drive a car)

7 _____
(past: live with his parents, now: live in an apartment)

8 _____
(past: not travel, now: go on holiday twice a year)

2c

Vocabulary

Feelings and reactions

1a Match words 1–8 with words and phrases a–h.

1 dull ....
2 homesick ....
3 anxious ....
4 lively ....
5 stressful ....
6 unpleasant ....
7 cheerful ....
8 peaceful ....

a feeling sad because you are not at home or with your family
b with a lot of energy
c not enjoyable
d not relaxing
e boring
f worried
g happy
h calm or quiet

b Complete the table with adjectives 1–8 from Exercise 1a.

Positive adjectives	Negative adjectives

2 Complete the missing adjectives.

1 I'm really n_____s about my exam. I don't think I've studied enough!
2 My new boss is really u_____t . She's very demanding and shouts a lot.
3 I felt really h_____k the whole time I was there. I really missed my family and friends!
4 He is quite o_____c about the whole thing. He thinks everything will go really well.
5 My uncle has three degrees and can speak five languages. He's an e_____y person.
6 It can be difficult to move to a new country. At first, everything can seem very s_____e.
7 I hoped the holiday would be exciting, but it was actually really d____l.
8 Having lunch with the guys from work is really e_____e. I have a good time with them.
9 Anna is such a c_____l person. I have never seen her without a smile on her face!
10 I had such a good time at my party last week. Everyone was dancing and laughing – it was really l_____y.

Grammar

so/ such ... that; too ... to; not ... enough to

3 Choose the correct alternatives.

1 I wonder if the course will be *too tough/ enough tough* for me?
2 It was *so/ such* a difficult year that he decided to return home.
3 There are *so/ such* many things I want to tell you that I don't know where to start.
4 We feel *so/ such* happy here that we're going to stay for another year!
5 I'm sorry I can't make it on Friday; I hope you aren't *too/ enough* disappointed.
6 He's had such an interesting life that we didn't have *time enough/ enough time* to ask him about everything.
7 Working in the office wasn't *enough exciting/ exciting enough* for me, so I quit!
8 I'm *such/ so* relaxed that I don't want to go back to work.

4 Match the sentence halves.

1 He felt so
2 It was such a
3 I didn't study
4 Living abroad wasn't exciting
5 They were too
6 I didn't have enough
7 I had such
8 There were so many

a enough for my exam, so I failed.
b angry that he threw the letter in the bin.
c terrible day that we decided to stay in.
d embarrassed to ask for directions.
e enough for me, so I moved home.
f a bad headache that I had to go to bed.
g people that I couldn't get a seat.
h money for a taxi, so I walked home.

Functional language

Show interest in a conversation

1 Complete the missing words in the conversations.

1 **A:** I had an interesting trip.
   B: W_____ happened?

2 **A:** In Africa I gave local children free classes.
   B: T_____ great!

3 **A:** I got lost in the forest – I was terrified.
   B: O_____ n_____!

4 **A:** So, I was walking home the other day …
   B: U_____ h_____ .

2 Choose the correct alternatives to complete the conversations.

1 **A** So I answered the phone and you'll never guess who it was!
   B _____ Go on.
   a <u>Uh huh.</u>   **b** Oh no!   **c** Wow!

2 **A** I had a really interesting meeting with my new boss today.
   B Really? _____
   a That's awful!   **b** What happened?   **c** Right.

3 **A** Laura told me that she's getting married. I'm so happy for her!
   B _____ That's fantastic news!
   a Oh no!   **b** And what happened next?   **c** Great.

4 **A** I've lost my wallet. I had it at the shops and now I can't find it anywhere.
   B _____ You should cancel your cards!
   a That's so cool!   **b** Wow!   **c** That's awful!

5 **A** And when I opened the door, I saw a strange man in my kitchen!
   B That's so frightening. _____
   a So, what did you do?   **b** That's amazing!
   c Great!

6 **A** Our holiday was a disaster. My bag was stolen on the first day and it had my passport in it.
   B That's terrible. _____
   a Uh huh.   **b** What happened in the end?
   c Right!

7 **A** My wife just won £200,000!
   B _____ Congratulations!
   a Wow!   **b** And what happened next?   **c** Oh no!

8 **A** Did I tell you I'm leaving the company?
   B _____? No, you didn't tell me!
   a Really   **b** Wow   **c** Right

9 **A** I missed my last train home yesterday, and it was raining really heavily.
   B Oh no, _____
   a uh huh.   **b** what did you do?   **c** right!

Listening

1 🔊 **2.01** **Listen to three people talking about their memories. Match descriptions 1–3 with the speakers: David (D), Holly (H) or Claudia (C).**

1 A life-changing experience _____
2 New tastes _____
3 A lucky escape _____

2 Listen again. Which sense does each person mention?
David: smell / sound / sight
Holly: smell / sound / sight
Claudia: smell / sound / sight

3 Listen again and choose the correct alternatives.

1 David and his brothers saw a herd of *cows/horses* running towards them.
2 David and his brothers felt *safe/shocked* when they reached their house.
3 *His brother/A smell* reminds David of that day.
4 Holly moved to China in *1988/1998*.
5 Holly *missed/didn't miss* her friends and family a lot in the beginning.
6 The *smell/colour* of rice soup reminds Holly of her time in China.
7 Claudia saw Rick Stevens when she was in her local *library/bookshop*.
8 Claudia is currently writing her *first/fourth* book.
9 A *book/song* reminds Claudia of that day.

Reading

1a Read the title of the article and look at the picture. Guess the correct alternatives.

1 Every day *seventy/ninety* percent of people remember something because of a sound, sight, taste or smell.

2 The brain is made of *100,000/1,000,000,000* neurons.

3 We should get at least *nine/seven* hours sleep at night.

b Read the article quickly and check your answers.

2 Read the article again. Are the sentences true (T) or false (F)?

1 Our senses help us to remember certain experiences, places and people. ....

2 Memories are stored in the hippocampus. ....

3 The action of remembering something is simple. ....

4 We only remember happy memories. ....

5 We always remember events exactly as they happened. ....

3 Read the article again and answer the questions.

1 What do *neurons* help the brain to do?

....

2 Where is the *hippocampus*?

....

3 Where is important information stored in the brain?

....

4 Why do we sometimes remember things which aren't true?

....

5 What is the best way to improve our memory?

....

6 What can we do to keep our memory active?

....

How does memory work?

Have you ever experienced a moment when a sound, sight, taste or smell made you feel happy or sad? Perhaps a song reminded you of something you used to do or somebody you used to know? Or maybe a specific sight or smell made you think of something you were doing at a particular time in the past? Everybody has experienced this at some time; in fact, nine out of ten people experience this at least once a day. Our senses are important in order to help us recall key moments, events and even people in our lives. But how does memory work? And why do we connect particular things with certain memories?

The brain is a complex part of our bodies; in fact, it is the most complex part we have! It is made of about a billion *neurons* and these help the brain to remember. The *hippocampus* is near the centre of the brain. It's responsible for keeping important memories and remembering where things are. It helps us remember the way to work, or where you left your keys.

The hippocampus is very busy. The action of remembering something is quite complicated! When your brain records memory, it usually records other details, such as where you were at the time, who you were with, and what you were eating. This explains why other small things, for example a certain smell or taste, can activate memories and make you think of something in the past.

Important information, like addresses and friends' names or things with a strong emotional connection, are stored in our long-term memory. In fact, we often connect feelings with memory. Feelings can have positive and negative effects on our memories; the sound of a song that makes you think of a happy moment or the sight of something that makes you feel frightened.

So can we trust our memory? Some memories are recorded better than others because of the large amount of information the hippocampus needs to process. However, sometimes when we remember, our brains can make small changes to the memory, mixing old memories with new details and changing it. This is why we sometimes think a particular event happened when it really didn't happen at all!

The best way to improve your memory is to keep it active. The more often you recall a memory, the easier it is to find! Doing exercise, getting at least seven hours sleep at night and developing new skills will keep your memory active and improve your ability to remember at any age!

Writing

1 Read the blog post and match the topics below with paragraphs A–D.

Get a better job!   ~~Independence~~   Learn a language
Make international friends

Taking a gap year

So, you've just finished school and you don't want to see another book for a while! What are your options? You could go to university or start work, but how about a gap year?

A _Independence_
If you take a year out and go somewhere on your own, you quickly learn how to look after yourself. If you travel alone, you have to think for yourself. Finding your way around a new city or country will mean working out the public transport system. For most students, living alone might be a new experience. Just finding a flat and managing your money will teach you independence. If you travel and live alone, there's no choice – you have to look after yourself!

B
Travelling around the world or volunteering abroad will mean that you meet new people from different places. When you travel alone, you tend to talk to more people. Being in similar situations brings people together and it's always more fun to share experiences when you're travelling with others. And it doesn't take much effort – just sitting next to someone on a bus or a train can lead to a friendship.

C
'How can a gap year improve my CV?' you might ask. A gap year shows initiative and a sense of adventure and independence. It also says to potential employers that you have cultural awareness. This is important in today's world of work. If you do some voluntary work or an internship and gain work experience along the way, even better!

D
A gap year normally means going abroad and learning a language. Why not try a country whose language you are interested in learning? The best way to learn a language is to be in the country where you can practise every day with local people. By shopping and speaking to locals you'll have the opportunity to use the language and make fast progress.

So what are you waiting for? Pack your rucksack and decide on where you would like to go!

2 Read the Focus box and choose the correct alternatives.

Writing paragraphs

A well-organised paragraph focuses on one [1]_sentence/ topic_.

Topic sentence
The first sentence of the paragraph usually gives the writer's main idea about the topic.
Life was certainly different in my grandparents' day.

Example sentences
The rest of the paragraph usually supports the main idea by giving [2]_examples/advice_, reasons and supporting details.
There were no modern appliances such as washing machines and vacuum cleaners to make housework easy, so they had to work hard to keep their house clean.

Conclusion sentence
A paragraph often finishes with a sentence that gives a result or conclusion.
Life was harder and less interesting.

3 Read the blog post again and underline the topic sentence in each paragraph. The first one is underlined for you.

Prepare

4 You're going to write a blog post about finding the perfect job. Use the headings below and make notes about what you will write in your topic sentences, and what examples/extra information you will give.
- Find what motivates you
- Choose the right company
- Be open-minded!

Write

5 Write your blog post. Use your notes in Exercise 4 and the example introduction and conclusion below to help you.

> Finding a job can be stressful, so think carefully about what is important to you when you begin looking for your ideal job.

> Whatever you decide, make sure that you think about all the factors above before you say yes. We spend so much time in our jobs, so it's important to be happy!

Vocabulary

Experiences

1 Choose the correct alternatives.

1 Gareth has been to so many places. He loves *experiencing/applying* new cultures and meeting new people.

2 It's been my dream since I was a child to *raise/perform* on stage. And this year, I'm going to do it!

3 Every January, people decide to *go on/take up* a new hobby. It doesn't always last though!

4 What achievement are you most proud of? I think *exploring/going on* the jungle of Borneo was the best thing I've ever done.

5 I've *applied/attended* to appear on the *Saturday Live* show. I hope they pick me!

6 They're *experiencing/going on* holiday next week, so they won't be able to come to the party. We'll miss them!

2 Complete the sentences with a suitable word or phrase.

1 A film star will r *aise* £100,000 for charity.

2 The team are going to e_____ the Amazon jungle in order to update our maps.

3 Thousands of people are going to take part i_____ the London Marathon this year.

4 I'd love to a_____ to be a film extra.

5 They are going to p_____ in a new musical this summer.

6 She left because she wanted to e_____ life in a new country.

7 I want to g_____ ice skating this weekend.

8 Lots of people are taking u_____ golf at the moment.

Grammar

Present perfect and past simple

3 Complete the sentences with the present perfect or past simple form of the verbs in brackets.

1 I _____saw_____ (see) Jonas at the shops last weekend and we agreed that we should all meet up again soon.

2 I _____ (not go) to that area before – is it nice?

3 I _____ (live) in Cambridge for five years, but then I got bored and decided to move to a bigger city.

4 We _____ (live) there for two years now, and we absolutely love it.

5 _____ you _____ (try) the seafood at the party last night? It was delicious, especially the prawns.

6 _____ you _____ (ever/see) her office? It's amazing – it's got such a brilliant view of the city skyline.

7 I'm not coming for lunch, I _____ (already/eat) something.

8 You want to talk to Clarissa? Sorry, she _____ (just/leave) and I'm not sure when she'll be back.

9 I _____ (not do) any exercise for a long time. I'm so unfit!

10 I've had Indian food at that place a few times. The last time _____ (be) amazing!

4 Put the words in the correct order to make sentences.

1 you / been / ever / Have / Dublin / to / ?

....

2 Grace / wanted / has / to explore / the Himalayas / always

....

3 been / several times / Berlin / I've / to

....

4 seen / yet / new / the / Have / you / Batman film / ?

....

5 They / her / been / haven't / yet / to visit

....

6 never / abroad / lived / I've

....

7 Luca / raised / £10,000 / for charity / already / has

....

8 performed / ever / in a play / she / Has / ?

....

5 Complete the text with *for* or *since*.

City escape

Are you adventurous? Have you lived in Valencia **1**_____ a long time? Have you wanted to be on TV **2**_____ you were a child? Have you wanted to try something new **3**_____ ages? Have you wanted to be famous **4**_____ years? If the answer is yes to any of those questions, this could be the right opportunity for you!

TV FIVE has been making great TV programmes **5**_____ 2010 and we're looking for people like you to apply for our new show. If you've been living in Valencia **6**_____ at least five years and can speak Spanish, then you could be suitable!

Email info@cityescape.uk and tell us why you should take part. We look forward to hearing from you!

Vocabulary

Keeping in touch/catching up

1 Match the phrases in the box with words/phrases 1–6 in the text with a similar meaning.

| catch up on ___ | get on well ___ | got to know ___ |
| hang out ___ | lose touch ___ | meet up with ___ |

Work has been really busy lately, so I don't have time to **¹see** my old friends. Normally, we always **²spend time** together at the weekends and **³talk about** all the news and gossip, but I just haven't had time recently. I really miss them and I don't want to **⁴stop communicating** with them. At the same time, I've **⁵become friends with** some of the people in the office, and we **⁶have a really good relationship**.

2 Choose the correct option a, b or c to complete the conversations.

1 **A:** Do you still meet up with Sara from time to time?
   B: Yes, we ___ each other these days.
   a see a lot of   **b** lose touch   **c** catch up

2 **A:** How often do you see Ed?
   B: Ed? I haven't seen him in years. We ___ when he moved to Germany and we haven't spoken since.
   a spent time   **b** lost touch   **c** caught up

3 **A:** Gemma! It's great to hear from you! We haven't met up in ages.
   B: I know! How about this weekend? We can hang out and ___ on all the news and gossip.
   a stay in touch   **b** catch up   **c** get together

4 **A:** Any plans for the weekend, Beth?
   B: Yes, we're going to ___ friends of ours for dinner and drinks.
   a meet up with   **b** hang out   **c** see a lot of

5 **A:** I love going out and meeting new people, don't you?
   B: Not really. I prefer spending time with my old friends. We ___ , so I don't need to make any new friends.
   a get to know   **b** split up   **c** get on well

6 **A:** What have you been doing since I last saw you, Jim?
   B: Just working. I'm so busy I don't have time to ___ with friends anymore.
   a hang out   **b** caught up   **c** introduce

7 **A:** Bye Tim, see you soon.
   B: Take care, and ___ in touch.
   a lose   **b** keep   **c** catch

8 **A:** Do you enjoy spending time with your sister?
   B: Yes, but she lives in France so we don't see ___ very often.
   a together   **b** each other   **c** a lot of

Grammar

Present perfect continuous and present perfect simple

3 Complete each sentence so it has a similar meaning to the first. Use the words in brackets.

1 I started working at nine. It's midday now, and I'm still working.
   I _have been working_ for three hours. (been)

2 What have I done today? Slept!
   I've ___ all day. (been)

3 We don't contact each other anymore.
   We ___ with each other. (lost touch)

4 The last time I saw Ania was in June.
   I ___ June. (since)

5 I'm staying at my friend's place at the moment, so I haven't had time to look at my emails.
   I ___ for the last few days, so I haven't had time to look at my emails. (been)

6 We go on holiday to Ireland every year.
   We ___ to Ireland for many years. (going)

7 I've reduced how many hours I work recently. I was often there until midnight!
   I ___ less time at work recently. Before, I was often there until midnight! (spending)

8 John? No, he's not here. I don't remember him coming in.
   I ___ this morning. (seen)

4 Correct the mistake in each sentence.

   have
1 What/~~are~~ you been doing since I last saw you?

2 This isn't the first time we have lose touch.

3 Nazir have been spending a lot of time with his friends recently.

4 They have just finish studying for their exams.

5 She have performed on stage since she was very young and now she is a professional dancer.

6 I have doing several courses in art this year.

7 We have to stayed in touch since he left.

8 I've be catching up with old friends recently.

9 I have been wait for you for thirty minutes.

10 I have been have nightmares recently.

3c

Vocabulary

Features of a town

1 Complete the quotes with the words in the box.

cycle lanes   landmark   outdoor café   skyline
suburb   traffic jams

1 My favourite thing to do in the evening is to look at the sun set over the city _____ .

2 It takes so long to get to work in the mornings because of the _____ .

3 If you do one thing when you get to Tokyo, visit the *Skytree*. You can't miss it. It's such a famous _____ .

4 No, I don't drive anymore. Now there are _____ it's safer to travel to work by bicycle.

5 It's so nice to sit outside and have a coffee in the sun at an _____ .

6 I don't want to live in the busy and crowded centre, give me a quiet _____ any day!

2 Cross out the incorrect alternative in each sentence.

1 The *neighbourhood/suburb/~~skyline~~* where I live is as interesting and historical as the city centre. I love to walk around the streets and have a coffee in the local cafés at the weekend.

2 What I love most about my city is how green it is! It's so easy to get around without a car with all of the *pedestrian streets/cycle lanes/traffic jams*.

3 When we visit new cities, we love to get out and explore. It's so much fun to visit the local *art galleries/landmarks/cycle lanes* and be a tourist for the day.

4 You could spend hours exploring this city. There is always something new to discover. With a large number of famous *squares/landmarks/cycle lanes*, Venice is one of the most popular cities in the world.

5 The one thing that surprises people when they come here is the view of the *skyline/main square/traffic jam*. It's spectacular.

6 It's all about culture and relaxation for Mike when he goes on a city break. You can't get him away from the *outdoor cafés/art galleries/skylines*.

Grammar

Articles

3 Correct the mistake in sentences 1–5.

People

1 ~~The people~~ use their phones too much these days – I don't think it's healthy.

2 Where did you put a key? I can't find it anywhere!

3 My brother's teacher – he loves it!

4 Paris skyline is so beautiful at night.

5 The money isn't important to me – I work hard because I love my job.

6 I live in the UK although I travel quite a lot for the work.

4 Complete the comments with *a, an, the* or no article (–).

The best cities in the world – as voted for by you

As **1**_____ tour guide, I've travelled all over **2**_____ world, but there is only one place I call home and that's Perth, **3**_____ capital of Western Australia. We've got everything here: **4**_____ beautiful beaches, lively bars and scenic parks. (Mark, Perth, Australia)

If I had to pick **5**_____ city, then Madrid would definitely be **6**_____ city at the top of my list! The bars and cafés are great when you want to get together with **7**_____ friends and hang out. And **8**_____ Spanish people are so open and friendly. (Emer, Madrid, Spain)

I'm **9**_____ New Yorker, and New York has **10**_____ great food and famous landmarks, but Houston is magical. Kids and adults alike will enjoy **11**_____ Houston Museum of Natural Science, and art lovers shouldn't miss the Art Car Museum. **12**_____ food is amazing! (Teresa, Houston, US)

Functional language
Ask for, follow and give directions

1 Put directions a–f in the correct order 1–6.

a Start at the theatre on Main Street. Go … *1*

b on down Wellington Street and then turn right ……

c along Main Street until you get to the bank. Turn ……

d at the supermarket. Go along Bute Street until you get to the library. Cross ……

e over the road at the library and the Tourist Information Centre is next to the bus station. ……

f left when you get to the traffic lights after you pass the bank. Go straight ……

2 Put the words in the correct order to complete the conversations.

1 **A:** Excuse me, can you tell me how to get to the library?

   B: road on / the left / Sure. Walk / this street, / and take / the first / along

     1 Sure. Walk along this street and take the first road on the left.

   A: OK.

   B: opposite / It's / park / the

     2 ………………………………………………

2 **A:** way / the quickest / What's / to Glen Street / ?

     3 ………………………………………………

   B: I'm not sure, actually. Try the tourist information office.

   A: there / get / How / I / do / ?

     4 ………………………………………………

   B: Sorry, I don't know. I'm new here.

3 **A:** Go straight on / is / on your / left / and / the swimming pool

     5 ………………………………………………

   B: I'm sure I went that way before…

   A: next to / It's / supermarket / a big

     6 ………………………………………………

   B: Oh! I know where it is, thank you!

4 **A:** Do you know where Gigi's Italian restaurant is?

   B: it's / Yes, / the theatre / across from

     7 ………………………………………………

   A: The theatre, I don't remember where that is … Is it far?

   B: It's / 15 minutes' / about / walk

     8 ………………………………………………

Listening

1 🔊 3.01 Listen to three people talking about how they have kept in touch with friends. Match statements a–c with speakers 1–3.

a It's easy to stay in touch if you want to. ……

b Friends come and go. ……

c Catching up with old friends is an annual tradition. ……

2 Listen again and answer the questions.

1 How many cities has speaker 1 lived in?

………………………………………………

2 Which group of friends are difficult for speaker 1 to meet?

………………………………………………

3 How many times a year does speaker 1 meet her childhood friends?

………………………………………………

4 How did speaker 2 use to communicate with friends?

………………………………………………

5 How does speaker 2 communicate with friends these days?

………………………………………………

6 Why did speaker 3 move around so much?

………………………………………………

7 How many friends does speaker 3 keep in touch with?

………………………………………………

8 Why does speaker 3 think that it's difficult to stay friends with people from her past?

………………………………………………

3a Which speaker 1–3:

a thinks some friendships can last forever? ……

b feels their life is not the same as some of their friends? ……

c thinks social media makes keeping in touch easy? ……

d thinks people are sometimes too lazy to keep in touch? ……

e feels that it's easy to be friends with people they work with? ……

f says we shouldn't feel too sad about losing friends? ……

b Listen again and check.

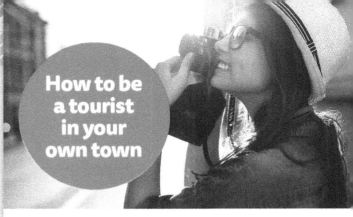

How to be a tourist in your own town

Reading

1 Read the article. What's it about? Choose the correct alternative a, b or c.

a saving money by staying at home

b rediscovering the place where you live

c the best places to visit in a city

2 Read the article again and answer the questions.

1 What two adjectives does the writer use to describe the hop-on hop-off bus?

....

2 Why does the writer recommend taking a notebook?

....

3 What 'romantic' activities does the writer suggest you can do in your city?

....

4 According to the writer, how do our busy lives affect our friendships?

....

5 Why does the writer recommend visiting an art gallery?

....

6 What advice does the writer give about taking photos?

....

....

3 Complete the summary of suggestions from the article.

1 Take a .... to see the sights! (tip 1)

2 Appreciate the views in your city at .... (tip 2)

3 We should make the time to catch up with .... (tip 3)

4 You can feel like you're on holiday if you do something .... from what you usually do. (tip 4)

5 Leave your .... at home so you can enjoy the moment! (tip 5)

4 Read the article again and find a word or phrase which means:

1 very close to where you live (tip 1)

....

2 a specific location/place (tip 2)

....

3 talking about what you've done recently (tip 3)

....

4 on holiday (tip 4)

....

5 taking photos quickly (tip 5)

....

When an economic crisis hits we tend to look closer to home for fun and adventure – and we might be surprised at what we discover. Here are five tips for how to reconnect with your hometown.

1 Take a tourist bus

When you visit a new place it's a good idea to get familiar with the city quickly and a hop-on hop-off bus is the quickest and most comfortable way to explore. But why not try it in your own city? How many places do you really know? You'll be amazed to discover what's on your doorstep. To enjoy the experience more, take a notebook and write down all the new places you find. Then when you get home or back to the office, you can impress everyone with fascinating facts about your city.

2 Make a date with your city

Making a date with your city may sound silly, but how often do you watch the sunset or stop and admire the buildings or monuments in your city? Think about all the tourists that arrive in coaches – they must be coming for something, right? It can be as simple as finding a spot where you can admire the skyline at sunset. Take a snack and a book and appreciate the view with the eyes of a tourist.

3 Reconnect with old friends and try out that restaurant

Make that dinner date! In the routine of work, family and other responsibilities, time passes and before you know it, you haven't seen your best friend for a year! If you take a break in your own city, you can make dates that you don't usually have time for. How many restaurants have opened in the last six months in your city? More than you would imagine. So, get the *What's On* guide and see what's new, book a table and meet up with that long-lost friend. An evening out catching up with a friend can be as good as a holiday!

4 Be a culture vulture for one day

Do something completely different. If you haven't seen much art before, go to an art gallery. If you don't know much about history, go to an exhibition at your local museum. Just breaking your routine can make you feel like you're away. You might even surprise yourself and find a new interest or find a new hobby you want to take up.

5 Leave your camera at home

When we travel, there's always the pressure of taking photos (to quickly post them on social media sites), but why do we have to photograph every street corner or monument we see? Maybe it's because you know you might not see it again. This doesn't happen in your own city. The city isn't going anywhere, so instead of worrying about snapping everything in sight, you can relax and enjoy the moment. So take a map, put on your tourist hat and go explore! You might just fall in love with your own city … again.

3

Writing

1 Read the text and match the headings in the box to paragraphs 1–4.

Eating and drinking   Culture   Parks   Shopping and coffee

HOME   ADVENTURES   DESTINATIONS   ABOUT   CONTACT

Visit Madrid!

The capital of Spain has something to offer every traveller. Here are some things to do in this amazing city.

1 ....
Salamanca is a fantastic neighbourhood where you'll find many fashionable boutique shops. There are lots of outdoor cafés too, so when you get tired from walking around the shops, you can stop for a relaxing drink. However be warned – Salamanca is more expensive than other neighbourhoods, but you don't have to spend money, you can just look!

2 ....
Lavapies is a very different neighbourhood from Salamanca, but when I travel I love to see the contrasts in a city. Here you'll find a few private galleries with some original pieces of art. There are also some interesting exhibitions, so make sure you get the *What's On* guide when you arrive so you don't miss anything.

3 ....
Retiro is a must if you are here on a Sunday, especially in warm weather. You'll find lots of activity here at the weekend but if you want to escape the crowds you can always hire a boat for an hour and cruise the central lake. This is the place for you if you need some green spaces and fresh air.

4 ....
Last but not least, there are some fabulous restaurants in every neighbourhood. Prices are reasonable for a city and there's a great variety of places to go, so if you enjoy your food, see my top five in the links below.

2 Read the Focus box. Do you think the text in Exercise 1 was written for tourists or people moving to Madrid?

Planning a piece of writing

When we plan a piece of writing, we start by thinking about the reader. What topic areas would they be interested in?

After that, we decide what order to put the topics in. Each topic should have a separate paragraph, so we can call this our 'paragraph plan'. Then we can make notes about each topic area to help us think about what to write.

Look at the examples below for a guide to a city:

Paragraph plan:
Paragraph 1: Introduction to the city
Paragraph 2: Must-see sights
Paragraph 3: Getting around
Paragraph 4: Shopping

Notes about the topic 'Getting around':
Taxis – expensive
Metro – cheap and quick
Boat trip – on river Avon

3 Look at the notes below and decide if they match the topic 'Culture' (C) or 'Shopping' (S).
1 some museums – free entry ....
2 markets every Sunday ....
3 great places to buy gifts ....
4 three great theatres in centre ....
5 visit world-famous opera ....
6 can find high-quality shoes, but not cheap ....

Prepare

4 You're going to write a travel blog recommending places of interest in a city. Make notes on the following:
- culture
- shopping
- parks
- eating and drinking
- getting around

Write

5 Write your blog post. Use your notes in Exercise 4 and the Focus box to help you.

Vocabulary
Lifestyles

1 **Match the adjectives in the box with the descriptions.**

easy-going   energetic   healthy   inactive   sensible   sociable   stressful   unhealthy

1 I need to do some exercise! I sit in front of my desk all day! _____

2 My flatmate is great. She never complains and doesn't worry about who cleans and cooks. _____

3 The problem is I love fast food and eat it three times a week. _____

4 My daughter is always out meeting new people. _____

5 City life is hard sometimes – people are always running around and it can get so noisy. _____

6 My three-year-old son doesn't stop – he's always doing something and can't sit still. _____

7 I eat plenty of fruit and vegetables. _____

8 I save some money every month in case I need it one day. _____

2 **Choose the correct alternatives.**

Modern living can be difficult. Can technology make it easier? Most of us have very ¹*busy/sociable* lifestyles. There's not much time to do the things we want to do. In some ways we are more ²*sociable/energetic* than previous generations. With technology, we're always available to friends and workmates. This can also be ³*stressful/active* because we are always connected on our phones and we can never take a break. However, I think we can be more ⁴*healthy/sensible* about how much time we spend on our phones. Is checking our messages every five minutes necessary or ⁵*healthy/energetic*? I believe that if we control our use of technology more, we can benefit from it. What's more, there are so many apps now that can help you improve your general fitness. For example, there are apps which count your steps and this can motivate you to be more ⁶*energetic/fun*. It's a very ⁷*simple/quiet* way of doing more exercise every day. If we use technology well, it can improve our quality of life.

Grammar
Comparatives

3 **Complete the sentences with the comparative form of the adjectives in brackets.**

1 Life is _more stressful_ (stressful) now because of busier lifestyles.

2 Life in the country is _____ (slow) than life in big cities.

3 In some ways, society is _____ (healthy) today.

4 Their diets are _____ (good) than ours because they eat so much more fish.

5 It is thought that children in the past did exercise _____ (regular) than children today. Lots of children are now also eating too much.

6 Some people say millennials are _____ (interested) in global issues than previous generations, because they care more about the planet.

7 Pollution is _____ (bad) in cities where there is more industry and traffic.

8 She cooks _____ (well) than me. Her curries are amazing.

9 Food in fast-food restaurants is often much _____ (fattening) than food prepared at home.

10 Because many people sit at a desk all day, they are _____ (active) than before.

4 **Put the words in the correct order to make sentences.**

1 eat out / It's healthier / than / to cook your own food
_____

2 more important / Health / is / than / work
_____

3 riding a bike / is / worse for the environment / Driving a car / than
_____

4 is less boring / than / I think working with other people / working alone
_____

5 than / Young people do exercise / more regularly / before
_____

6 less money / I don't mind / if / earning / I'm happy
_____

7 buying houses today / fewer people / than / There are / in previous generations
_____

8 is not as / Life in the country / life in the city / stressful as
_____

5 **Rewrite the sentences using the words in brackets so that they mean the same.**

1 Skiing is not as dangerous as snowboarding.
Snowboarding is _____ than skiing. (more)

2 Traffic is worse now than in the past.
Traffic in the past wasn't as _____ it is now. (bad)

3 There are fewer people living in villages.
There aren't as _____ people living in villages. (many)

4 Sue couldn't swim as well as Kat.
Kat could swim _____ Sue. (better)

5 Our service is generally better than other services.
Other services are generally not _____ as ours. (good)

Vocabulary

Products and services

1 **Choose the correct alternatives.**

1 *Environmentally friendly/Easy to use* products are products which are good for our planet.

2 Excellent *service/use* keeps customers very happy.

3 *Good value/Well designed* products work very well because people have thought carefully about them.

4 Poor *quality/value* products are ones which are not made very well, often because they are made cheaply.

5 *Easy to use/Good value* products don't need millions of instructions.

6 *Good value/Reliable* products are worth their price.

7 A *reliable/good value* product performs well and consistently without failing or breaking.

2 **Complete the reviews with the phrases in the box.**

easy to use   environmentally friendly
excellent service   good value   high quality
poor quality   poorly designed   reliable
well designed

1 It looked nice but the material was very
....

2 I always buy .... products.
We need to protect the planet.

3 It doesn't work the way they say it does. This product is
.... , don't buy it!

4 They're such .... tables – the material they use is excellent.

5 I can recommend my new mobile phone company. They are very friendly and offer a really
....

6 Sue is the best! She's always there when you need her. She's very.. .

7 I'm a little scared of technology, but this product was so .... – I managed to get it working in minutes!

8 For the price, this product is amazing – It's really
....

9 This website is a really .... site – everything is very clear.

Grammar

Superlatives

3 **Complete the conversations with the superlative form of the adjectives in brackets.**

1 A: You know, I think this is the [1] __*nicest*__ (nice) phone I've ever had.

B: I need a new one, actually. Mine is definitely the [2] .... (bad) phone I've had. It's always turning itself off!

2 A: How was your weekend away, Jo? The place looked amazing. I saw your comment saying it was the [3] .... (good) holiday you've had, so I guess it was good!

B: Oh, it really was, Sam. The service was excellent. I think the hotel staff were the [4] .... (friendly) I've ever met.

3 A: Well, for me, the [5] .... (+ important) thing about a washing machine is its reliability.

B: Yes, I agree. I think the [6] .... (– important) thing is the brand name. There are some excellent products out there which aren't well-known names.

4 A: Hey – have you seen the new car ad on TV? It's probably the [7] .... (funny) one I've ever seen.

B: Yes! I saw it last night. It's very clever advertising, don't you think?

A: Definitely. That's why they're one of the [8] .... (popular) brands.

4 **Correct the mistake in each sentence.**

    the
1 This is easiest route to the city centre.

2 This must be the louder washing machine I've ever had!

3 This restaurant is best in town – everyone knows it!

4 Why did you buy the cheaper one? You know it's going to be poor quality.

5 The most better phones come with good cameras.

6 I've always bought this brand. It's simply the most reliablest.

7 This is the baddest meal I've ever had – I want to speak to the manager.

8 I'm going for this one. I think it's the better value.

Vocabulary

Types of film

1 Complete each opinion with the type of film it describes. One letter is given.

1 I love this film. It's a classic r<u>omantic comedy</u> where two heroes end up falling in love and getting together – after some problems, of course.

2 This was a very sad film. Based on real events in the Second World War, it tells the story of a few individuals. In some parts, it felt like a _ _ c _ _ _ _ _ _ _ _ because it was so realistic.

3 I had my eyes closed for most of the film. If you like _ _ _ _ _ r, this is the film for you. But I warn you now – there's a lot of blood.

4 This was the most exciting _ _ t _ _ _ film I've ever seen. It was so fast moving that when the film ended I couldn't believe two hours had passed!

5 I don't normally like f _ _ _ _ _ _, but this was such a beautiful story with lots of princesses, monsters and magic.

6 My children loved this _ _ _ _ _ t _ _ _. In fact, I enjoyed it, too. It was very funny in parts.

2 Use the clues to complete the crossword.

Across
2 a funny film which will make you laugh
3 _____-fiction – a film based on the future and often set in space
6 a film about real events and facts

Down
1 _____-comedy – a film about love ... with humour!
4 a film with mystical characters
5 a scary film which makes you jump
6 a serious film with realistic characters
7 a film with song and dance

Grammar

Defining relative clauses

3 Complete the descriptions with the correct relative pronoun.

1 This is a story of a young girl [1] _____who_____ begins to act very strangely. At the beginning of the film she is a normal child but she quickly becomes rude and starts using bad language. The scene [2] _____ she starts to fly is really scary!

2 This is a story of a thirty-something woman [3] _____ gets into lots of trouble. It became very popular all over the world. *Bridget Jones* tells the story of a woman [4] _____ life is always a little crazy. It's a classic romantic comedy [5] _____ will have you laughing all the way to the end.

3 This biopic tells the story of how King George VI came to the throne. Colin Firth is a king [6] _____ needs help from a speech therapist so he can give a speech [7] _____ will change history.

4 This film takes you to an exciting world [8] _____ everything is very different. The sound effects and images are awesome! The story is about a girl [9] _____ is looking for her father, and tells the story of all the strange things [10] _____ happen to her.

4 Complete the sentences with the correct relative pronoun.

which/that

1 The film cost the most to make was *Spaceplanes*.

2 He's an actor has appeared in many films.

3 It's a moving film tells the story of a young boy growing up in India.

4 I think it's a film will be popular with all ages.

5 She plays a woman husband is a criminal.

6 It's the famous scene Harry meets Sally.

7 The film is set in a city there are many problems.

8 I like actors are believable.

Functional language
Ask for and give opinions

1 Choose the correct alternatives.

1 What did you think of *him/he*?
2 It was *amazing/awful*! I loved it!
3 I *found/thought* it boring.
4 It was OK, I *know/guess*.
5 Best book I've read in *much time/ages*.
6 It's good but not her *best/better*.
7 I was a bit *disappointed/disappoint*.
8 I thought he was *really/a lot* good.

2 Complete the phrases with the words in the box.

> ages   found   honest   kind   really   what   bit
> thought

1 _____ did you think of it?
2 It's not my _____ of thing.
3 I thought it was awful, to be _____ .
4 I _____ it a bit boring.
5 I _____ enjoyed it.
6 Best film I've seen in _____ .
7 Jo liked the film, but I _____ it was strange.
8 I liked the book, but it was a _____ long.

3 Complete the conversation with phrases a–f.

A: So, did you watch that new BBC series last night?
B: Yes and I loved it – ¹ _d_ !
A: It was good, but ² _____ . I think I preferred the other one we watched together.
B: Really? I ³ _____ it – I couldn't stop watching.
A: I wasn't crazy about the actress ... what's her name ... ? I found her a bit annoying, to be honest.
B: Didn't you like her? I'm surprised. I thought she ⁴ _____ . I've never seen her in anything before.
A: I'll watch the next episode anyway. Maybe I need to give it a second chance. The thing is, I ⁵ _____ – nothing really happened.
B: Ah, but I think the next one will be more exciting.
A: Maybe.
B: Oh and ⁶ _____ of the scenery? I thought it was absolutely stunning.
A: Oh yes. I have to admit that was impressive!
B: Ha! I thought you would appreciate that, at least. I think they filmed it in Canada – I really want to visit now!

a   not the best
b   was really good
c   what did you think
d   it was amazing
e   really enjoyed
f   found it a bit boring

Listening

1 🔊 **4.01 Listen to five people talking about things they couldn't live without and match speakers 1–5 with objects A–E.**

1 Luke _____   a computer
2 Amy _____   b walking boots
3 Paul _____   c book
4 Jo _____   d online shopping
5 Clem _____   e phone

2 Listen again and complete the interview notes.

Luke

1 Luke uses his phone to _listen to music_ .
2 Luke listens to music on his way to the office and _____ .
3 Luke needs music because he lives in a place which is _____ .

Amy

4 If Amy went to a desert island, she wouldn't take _____ .
5 If Amy needs a break, she _____ .
6 Amy's biggest interest is _____ .

Paul

7 Paul uses his laptop for scheduling, talking to people and _____ .
8 Paul's laptop is important to him because it helps him _____ .
9 Paul spends a lot of time _____ .

Jo

10 Jo likes Netline Direct because she can use it from home and _____ .
11 Jo was very happy with the customer service because _____ .
12 Jo buys things for herself, and she also buys _____ .

Clem

13 Clem reads for a minimum of _____ .
14 Wherever she goes, she _____ .
15 The last book she read was called _____ .

Reading

1 **Read the posts quickly and match topics a–e with paragraphs 1–5.**

a Home delivery ....
b Learning ....
c TV choices ....
d More shopping choice ....
e Social life ....

1 We've advanced so much in education since I started teaching in the '80s and it's mostly thanks to technology. I have an interactive whiteboard and learning is much more interesting. Of course, there are always disadvantages. I often get messages from colleagues at the weekend about new teaching policies or questions about marking! In addition, technology is not 100% reliable, but for me, there are more pros than cons. I enjoy teaching much more today.
A grateful teacher, 50

2 We have more choice now with shops. I do everything online; from booking holidays to buying clothes and food shopping. It makes my day-to-day life much easier because we are a family of five and there's always so much to buy. Now I have everything pre-ordered, so with a click of a button all my groceries for the week are sent and delivered in 24 hours – so simple! My life would be much more stressful without these services that didn't exist 20 years ago. I don't know how my mother managed!
A working mum, 47

3 I've lived and worked abroad for 20 years and catching up with friends and family is so important. We don't always speak on the phone, but sometimes a message is enough. Communication is so simple these days. Wherever you are in the world you can be in contact with your loved ones and this, for me, is really important. I also think there's more opportunity to meet people. We're sociable, but in a very different way from our grandparents.
A travel lover, 38

4 I've worked in the entertainment industry for many years and it has changed a lot — mostly for the good. I do worry a little about the future of entertainment, however. The quality and choice available has improved in so many ways, but people are choosing to watch series over films, which is a worry. We don't want to lose our cinemas. Today, I think there are a range of genres of programmes, so everyone can find something they like. This is definitely positive.
A modern traditionalist, 60

5 In my local supermarket there are six brands of coffee! It makes choosing difficult, so I'm not sure all this choice is positive – I spend longer at the supermarket than I used to. However, I do enjoy the great range we have nowadays and I wouldn't go back! I also think because there are so many different brands, products are of a higher quality than when I was younger. Online reviews also mean that companies and services have to be very careful, but I'm not sure that all this has improved customer service. You either get excellent or awful service. There's definitely more quality control today and the consumer has much more power than before.
A forward-thinking 70-year-old

2 **Read the posts again. Are the sentences true (T) or false (F)?**

1 The new teaching policies are an example of the positive impact of new technology in education. (paragraph 1) ....

2 Everyday life is easier. Now you can do all your shopping from your computer. (paragraph 2) ....

3 We are sociable, but not in the same way as before. (paragraph 3) ....

4 In terms of entertainment, people are going to the cinema now more than ever. (paragraph 4) ....

5 More choice means sometimes our shopping takes longer. (paragraph 5) ....

3 **Read the posts again and identify which of the writers 1–5 expresses ideas a–h.**

1 A grateful teacher
2 A working mum
3 A travel lover
4 A modern traditionalist
5 A forward-thinking 70-year-old

a We have more choice these days. .... , ...

b You can buy better quality things these days. ....

c The way things have changed might be bad for one industry. ....

d You can always be in contact with family and friends. ....

e It's not always good that people can communicate with you. ....

f It's easier to make new friends. ....

g Customers are in a stronger position than they were before. ....

h New technologies help people with busy lives. ....

4

Writing

1a Read the biography. Match topics 1–5 with paragraphs A–E.

1 Early life _____
2 Work/achievements _____
3 Education _____
4 Health _____
5 Death _____

A Born on 8th January 1942 in Oxford, England, Steven Hawking was a British scientist whose work has helped to make science accessible to everybody. As a boy, his dad wanted him to become a doctor, **but** Steven really wanted to study mathematics.

B He went to university in Oxford where he studied physics. His teachers described him as an extraordinary student. Later, he moved to Cambridge **because** he wanted to study cosmology. **However**, at the age of 21, doctors discovered he had a disease that would reduce his ability to speak and walk, and they said that he only had two years to live.

C **Although** his health got worse and eventually he was unable to walk, he lived an active and productive life and had a lot of success as a scientist and author, studying how time and space are related. Eventually, he was unable to speak, **so** he communicated through a computer.

D His health problems did not stop him, however, and he made important discoveries as well as being a very successful college lecturer. **In addition** to this, he wrote many important books on space and the universe, which helped the public or non-scientists to understand how the universe works. His most popular book, *A Brief History of Time*, sold over 10 million copies and was translated into more than 30 languages.

E He died on 14th March 2018. **As a result of** his work, he will always be an inspiration to people everywhere and one of the most famous scientists of the twenty-first century. The story of his life was told in the biopic *The Theory of Everything*.

b Read the biography again. Match the linkers in bold with the rules.

1 To show how one event is different from another, use _____ / _____ / _____ .

2 To add information, use _____ .

3 To show the reason for something, use _____ .

4 To show the result of something, use _____ .

c Read the Focus box and check your answers. Notice how and where we use these linkers in a sentence.

Using linkers

Use *although*, *but* and *however* to show how one event is different from another.
Although *his health got worse he lived an active and productive life.*
As a boy, his dad wanted him to become a doctor, ***but*** *Steven really wanted to study mathematics.*
However*, at the age of 21, doctors discovered he had a disease that would reduce his ability to speak and walk.*

Use *in addition (to)* to add information.
In addition to *this, he wrote many important books on space and the universe.*

Use *because* to show the reason for something.
Later, he moved to Cambridge ***because*** *he wanted to study cosmology.*

Use *as a result of*, *so* to show the result of an action.
As a result of *his work, he will always be an inspiration to people everywhere.*
Eventually, he was unable to speak, ***so*** *he communicated through a computer.*

2 Complete the biography with the linkers in the box.

as a result   because   but   however   in addition   so

My great-grandmother has always been an inspiration to me. She moved to Johannesburg when she was 15 [1] _____ she wanted to become a doctor. She didn't have a lot of money, [2] _____ she worked part time in an office.
She worked very hard and when she wasn't working, she spent all of her time studying. [3] _____ , she passed her exams. She was accepted into university to study a degree in medicine when she was only 17, [4] _____ her family were not happy. They wanted her to return home and get married. [5] _____ , she didn't and she stayed in university.
She followed her dream and finally she graduated from university and became one of the first female surgeons in the country. [6] _____ to this, she published three books and had seven children! I hope that one day I will be as successful as she was!

Prepare

3 You're going to write a biography of somebody important to you – a celebrity, a person from history or a family member. Make notes about their life:

- early life
- education
- work/achievements
- importance to you

Write

4 Write the biography. Use your notes in Exercise 3 to help you.

Vocabulary
Describing clothes and appearance

1 **Choose the correct alternatives.**

FASHION AND STYLE

Looking fashionable – style tips!

Are you tired of your old clothes?
Are you still wearing clothes from 10 or 20 years ago?
Is your style ¹*loose/old-fashioned* and outdated?
Do you want to try something new?
Try our tips below to look fashionable for less!

● Do you still wear the same colour bag, shoes and clothes? Well, it's time to stop! ²*Matching/Tight* clothes and shoes is not fashionable any more. It's time for some new clothes!

● Do you spend most of your time in big, comfortable ³*loose/tight* clothes? If so, then maybe it's time to buy some smart clothes, even if it's just for the office. Remember, your appearance is important.

● Finally, it's time to buy a good pair of jeans. Jeans can be worn in smart or ⁴*old-fashioned/casual* situations and are an essential part of everybody's wardrobe.

---

2 **Complete the missing words.**

1 I like wearing casual, sporty clothes, but sometimes I enjoy wearing something s_____ , too.

2 On Sundays I wear whatever I like. I don't care about what I've g_____ o_____ .

3 That dress is a little o_____ -f_____ for me, I prefer something a little more modern.

4 My mum goes crazy when I don't wear m_____ socks! I just like wearing two different colours.

5 If I wear things which are too t_____ , I sometimes can't breathe! It's uncomfortable.

6 My sister is really f_____ . She's always reading style magazines to find out what's coming next.

3 **Match the sentence halves.**

1 She thinks she's stylish, but _____
2 You'll recognise Pedro. He's _____
3 If you're flying, wear loose _____
4 You see a lot of fashionable _____
5 He looks strange in smart _____

a clothes – they'll be more comfortable.
b actually her clothes are old-fashioned.
c people on the streets of Paris and London.
d got yellow jeans on.
e clothes. I always see him wearing really casual stuff.

Grammar
Modal verbs: possibility and deduction

4 **Choose the correct alternatives to complete the sentences.**

1 You can't find your wallet? Oh no!
It _____
a mustn't be in the office.   b might be in the office.
c might not be in the office.

2 I don't know Richard well, but he
_____
a could not be really nice.   b can't be really nice.
c seems to be really nice.

3 I'm really busy, so I _____
a must come tonight.   b may come tonight.
c might not come tonight.

4 He's been in bed all day.
He _____
a can't be tired.   b may not be tired.
c can be tired.

5 They aren't answering the door.
They _____
a can't be out.   b may be out.
c don't seem out.

6 Alex always looks smart and fashionable.
He _____
a must have a good job.
b can have a good job.
c can't have a good job.

7 Why don't we go to the party at the weekend?
It _____
a could be a lot of fun.   b can't be a lot of fun.
c may not be a lot of fun.

8 That group of people are speaking Spanish.
I'm not sure, but they _____
a can't be from Argentina.
b must be from Argentina.
c may be from Argentina.

5 **Correct the mistake in each sentence.**

1 They may ~~to~~ be our friends, Jim and Rita, but I can't really see from here.

2 Lisandros seems being very confident about the interview tomorrow, but I know he's nervous.

3 I don't believe it – she can't to be 50 – she looks so young!

4 We don't might be able to come tomorrow.

5 People must to know about it because it's in all of the newspapers!

6 She coulds be from France but I'm not sure. She speaks English so well that it's impossible to know!

Vocabulary

Places to live

1 Match words 1–5 with definitions a–e.

1 block of flats ....
2 cottage ....
3 detached house ....
4 terraced house ....
5 studio ....

a a small flat or apartment
b a house that isn't joined to another house
c a house that's part of a group or row of similar houses
d a large building divided into flats
e a small house in the country

2 Complete the adverts with the words in the boxes.

air conditioning   central heating   detached   patio

1 .... **house for sale in Cardiff, Wales.**

Located very close to the centre of the city, this four-bedroomed house is not to be missed! A spacious and well designed house, it has three bathrooms, a large back garden with a **2** .... and a garage. The house also has incredible views onto Roath Park and Lake.

It comes with **3** .... to keep you cool in the summer months and **4** .... to keep you warm in the winter.

Call us now to book a viewing as this property is certain to sell quickly.

balcony   block of flats   ceilings   floors   studio

To rent, a **5** .... **in a great location.**

Modern and smart, this is a great option for anyone working in the city. It's located in a new **6** ...., right next to a bus stop and is only a five-minute walk to the train station.

Fully furnished and with a well equipped kitchen and bathroom, the walls and **7** .... have been painted recently, and the wooden **8** .... are completely new. It also has a very big **9** .... that offers great views of the city skyline.

Email us now to book your appointment to see this unique home.

Grammar

Zero and first conditional

3 Match the sentence halves.

1 If I'm tired,
2 I don't feel nervous
3 If we don't go to France,
4 I won't sleep well
5 If the train is delayed,

a I'll tell her that we'll be late.
b if I need to make a big speech.
c if I eat too much before bed.
d I'll stay home tonight.
e we might go to Egypt.

4 Complete the email with the correct form of the verbs in brackets.

Hi Mickey,

Thanks for your email. It's good to hear that you finally found a place to live. You've been looking for ages! The studio you found sounds perfect for one person. When you **1** .... (live) alone, you **2** .... (not need) a lot of space.

Mark and I moved into our cottage last month. I can't believe we finally own our own home. The house is beautiful and we love living in the country. It has a large back garden with a lot of flowers. When we **3** .... (have) more time, we **4** .... (build) a patio to have barbecues in the summer. If you **5** .... (come) to see it, you **6** .... (not be) disappointed.

Good luck with the move, it can be quite stressful! If you **7** .... (be) organised, I'm sure you **8** .... (be) fine. My advice is to do it at the weekend and make sure you have enough boxes!

I have rule. Every time I **9** .... (get) stressed out when I'm moving house, I **10** .... (take) a break for ten minutes. Try and do the same!

Write soon,
Laura

Vocabulary
Describing food

1 Match the sentence halves.

1 This coffee is _____
2 Mm, I don't want ice cream today, _____
3 I'm not having the curry if it's _____
4 Bread from the shop is fine, but _____
5 I really like **fried** fish – _____

a it's not the same when it's **grilled**.
b I prefer it when it's **homemade**.
c really **bitter**. Don't buy it again!
d I'd prefer something **savoury**.
e too **spicy**. It always makes me feel bad.

2 Cross out the alternative that is not possible in each sentence.

1 I know it's not very healthy, but I love foods that are *fried/cooked/~~spicy~~* in butter and fat.
2 Daniel has to have his coffee *strong/bitter/cooked* first thing in the morning.
3 I'd like the lamb, and for my friend the *spicy/grilled/bitter* chicken.
4 I don't like anything that tastes too *sweet/salty/grilled*.
5 My sister loves *hot/spicy/sweet* dishes – she'd eat curry every night if she could!
6 I don't eat a lot of *savoury/sweet/roast* snacks. Eating between meals is bad for you.
7 I like it because it's so *light/tasty/fried*.
8 My mum's *homemade/bitter/sweet* apple pie was always a favourite.

3 Complete the review with the words in the box.

> bitter   fried   grilled   homemade   savoury   spicy   sweet   tasty

Aled's Restaurant

⊙⊙⊙⊙○   Reviewed 3 weeks ago

Aled's is the first restaurant to be opened in the city by the successful head chef, and everyone is excited! Aled started his career working in restaurants abroad. He's become famous for using spices in his dishes and his amazing [1] _____ pies and sweet cakes.

The restaurant is located in the centre of the city and inside it's spacious and modern. To start, I ordered a green salad with [2] _____ bread baked that day. I really enjoyed it and it was really [3] _____ . For my main course, I ordered fish [4] _____ in olive oil and [5] _____ potatoes, and my friend had the curry. I was so jealous as it was simply amazing! For dessert, we ordered the lemon tart and chocolate cake as we both love [6] _____ food. Finally we ordered coffee. I thought it was slightly strong and [7] _____ , but my friend loved it!

Everything was delicious. As well as good food, the service at Aled's is excellent. So if hot, [8] _____ curry dishes are a favourite of yours, then Aled's won't disappoint!

Grammar
Quantifiers

4 Tick (✓) the correct sentences.

1 a We don't have some eggs – we need to buy them. _____
  b We don't have any eggs – we need to buy them. _____

2 a You should eat plenty fresh fruit and vegetables. _____
  b You should eat plenty of fresh fruit and vegetables. _____

3 a I like a little of sugar in my coffee. _____
  b I like a bit of sugar in my coffee. _____

4 a Doctors say you shouldn't eat a lot of sweets. They are bad for you! _____
  b Doctors say you shouldn't eat much sweets. They are bad for you! _____

5 a We don't eat no snacks between breakfast and dinner. _____
  b We don't eat any snacks between breakfast and dinner. _____

6 a How much cheese do you eat? _____
  b How many cheese do you eat? _____

7 a I drink a few coffee, but I can't drink a lot of it. It makes me nervous! _____
  b I drink a little coffee, but I can't drink a lot of it. It makes me nervous! _____

8 a Did you buy bread enough for dinner? _____
  b Did you buy enough bread for dinner? _____

5 Complete the missing words in the text messages.

> How [1]m *uch* _____ cereal do we have? Can you check? I think we still have a [2]b _____ of coffee, so I won't get [3]a _____ today.

> Mum! I forgot my lunch and I don't have [4]e _____ food to eat. I only have a [5]f _____ biscuits that I took this morning.

> We aren't vegetarians, but we don't eat [6]m _____ meat. I'm on a diet, too, so I don't want to eat too [7]m _____ chocolate or ice cream. See you later!

> I'll be there in five minutes! Can you order me a coffee? You know how I like it, with [8]l _____ of sugar!

Functional language
Give instructions and ask for information

1 Complete the recipe with the correct words.

1 F_____ of all, wash all the ingredients.
2 T_____, chop the cucumber and tomato and put in a bowl.
3 N_____, mix in olive oil, vinegar and garlic.
4 F_____, add feta cheese, salt and pepper and mix together.
5 T_____ it! Enjoy!

2 Put the the recipe in the correct order.

a That's it! Serve with a little olive oil and basil. _____
b While the base is cooking in the oven, prepare some toppings like olives or peppers. _____
c First, make the base with flour, water, yeast and salt. __1__
d Next, take out the pizza after 10 minutes and spread on your tomato sauce. _____
e Then, mix the tomato sauce, garlic and herbs, and put the base in the oven. _____
f Finally, add cheese, sliced tomato and your toppings. _____

3 Complete the telephone conversation with the phrases in the box.

> could you tell me   First of all   How long does that take
> Is there anything else   No, that's it   OK, go on   OK, I've got that

A: Hi Becky, sorry to bother you, but **1**_____ how to make your baked camembert? It was amazing!
B: Oh, it's so easy, Jane. Have you got a pen?
A: Yes, go ahead.
B: **2**_____, heat your oven to 200C. Take the cheese out of the plastic, but then put it back in the box it came in.
A: You mean, put the box in the oven?!
B: Yes, but don't worry it won't burn!
A: **3**_____. Put ... box ... in ... oven.
B: So, yes, you put the cheese in its box in the oven.
A: **4**_____?
B: Twenty minutes but, oops sorry, I forgot something ...
A: **5**_____.
B: Before you put the cheese in the oven, add some chilli.
A: OK and is that it? **6**_____?
B: **7**_____! Just serve it with some nice bread!

Listening

1 🔊 5.01 Listen and match topics a–c with conversations 1–3.

a Diets _____
b Appearances _____
c Moving house _____

2 Listen again and match conversations 1–3 with summaries a–c.

a One speaker complains about things they had to do while the other one mostly listens. _____
b The speakers disagree about something. _____
c One speaker persuades the other to do something. _____

3a Listen to conversation 1 again and answer the questions.

1 What is going to change in their office?
_____
2 Why does the man think it's a good change?
_____
3 Why does the woman disagree?
_____
4 What does the woman decide to do in the end?
_____

b Listen to conversation 2 again. Are the sentences true (T) or false (F)?

1 The man has been ill. _____
2 He's bought a flat in the city centre. _____
3 The woman knows how the man is feeling. _____
4 He's had problems with the house. _____

c Listen to conversation 3 again and put the summary in the correct order.

a Tina explains that she can't come. _____
b Gill tries to persuade Tina. _____
c Gill invites Tina to lunch. _____
d Tina explains a problem she has. _____
e Tina agrees to come. _____
f Gill gives Tina advice. _____

Reading

1 **Read the article and choose the best title.**
  a Mealtimes from around the world
  b Breakfasts from around the world
  c Superfoods from around the world

2 **Read the article again and answer the questions.**
  1 What drink is popular with breakfast in India?

  2 Which country has lots of meat-free options?

  3 Why is breakfast a simple meal in Spain?

  4 What does the writer recommend trying as part of breakfast in Spain?

  5 In Wales, what breakfast ingredient is from the sea?

  6 According to the article, how is the laverbread cake cooked?

  7 In Japan, what is usually eaten for breakfast if people don't have a lot of time in the morning?

  8 According to the article, why is breakfast so important?

3 **Find words and phrases in the article to match definitions 1–6.**
  1 Typical of something that has been done by a society or group of people for a long time. (paragraph 1)

  2 with lots of different types of things (paragraph 2)

  3 space for a particular thing (paragraph 3)

  4 A food that is used as part of a recipe, dish or meal. (paragraph 4)

  5 includes (paragraph 5)

  6 continues to be the same (paragraph 6)

1 What do you eat first thing in the morning? The first and – according to some people – most important meal of the day means different things for different people in countries around the world. Below, we look at some of our favourite traditional breakfasts eaten all over the world.

INDIA

2 Known for its cuisine, India has a rich and varied menu when it comes to meals and breakfast is no different. A typical breakfast in India will depend on the region and is different from north to south, but we've picked some of our favourites. Breakfast itself can be spicy and vegetarian options are common. *Chai*, or tea, is a popular option with breakfast. Breads such as *roti* or *dosas* are served with different yoghurt dips and fruit chutneys. Spiced potatoes, rice, vegetables and stuffed pancakes are other common options. With so much choice, it's difficult to decide what to have!

SPAIN

3 Breakfast in Spain is an important but simple affair, as you have to have room for lunch! Options include tortilla, a tasty omelette made of eggs and potato or *pan con tomate*, a toasted bread roll with olive oil, tomatoes and sometimes ham. Loved by both adults and children, and very popular with visitors, hot chocolate and *churros* – a sweet pastry to be dipped in your hot chocolate – is another possible choice. Not to be missed, however, is the *café con leche* – a strong cup of espresso with hot milk. If you try it, you won't be disappointed!

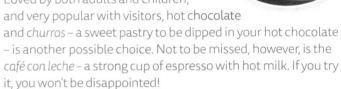

WALES

4 As well as fried foods such as eggs, sausages and bacon, a laverbread cake is a traditional addition to the breakfast menu in many parts of Wales. The key ingredient of the laverbread cake is seaweed, collected from the sea and boiled. This is then mixed with oats and fried in butter. A savoury morning treat and a healthy option, too!

JAPAN

5 Japanese food is famous around the world and breakfast doesn't disappoint! Breakfast is usually quite light and the traditional Japanese breakfast consists of a piece of grilled fish, miso soup and rice (sometimes served with a raw egg) and must be one of the healthiest on our list. Sometimes, if people need to be quick, toast and a green salad is eaten instead. Green tea or coffee are popular drinks with breakfast.

6 The list goes on and on! But while the food eaten for breakfast changes from country to country, it remains the most important meal of the day. It gives us routine and helps us form good habits, and is also part of our cultural traditions and customs. So the next time you're in a hurry, remember to take time for breakfast!

5

Writing

1a Choose the correct alternatives.

> ● ● ●
>
> Hi John,
>
> How's it going?
>
> I thought I would write and give you our news, as we haven't spoken ¹*for ages/first of all*. We've finally moved after living in a very small studio for years, and we've got a new place which is totally ²*awesome/anyway*.
>
> ³*So/Let me know*, the new place is a two-bedroom flat in a new block of flats. It has a huge balcony, which is great, as it means we can invite our friends to ⁴*be in touch/get together* at our place. Plus, I can now start my day with a cup of coffee on the balcony now that spring has arrived.
>
> ⁵*Anyway/Actually*, how is the new job? Are you happier now you've left that horrible stressful one you had before?
>
> If you're not ⁶*doing anything/free*, let's meet up soon. I ⁷*demand/fancy* a chat and a coffee.
>
> Speak soon,
> Theresa

b Complete the email with the phrases in the box.

> ages   Anyway   awesome   Do you fancy it
> have you been in touch   let me know   Speak soon

> ● ● ●
>
> Hi Heathcliff,
>
> How's life in Istanbul? The photos you sent look amazing!
>
> Jane and I have been thinking about meeting up in a city in Europe for a weekend break. We haven't had a holiday for a long time and it would be really nice if you could join us. ¹_____? I think it would be amazing, but ²_____ what you guys think.
>
> By the way, ³_____ with Kate? I know you said it was very difficult for her when she first arrived. I imagine it takes time to adapt to a new country. It would be ⁴_____ to go and see her there when I have the money.
>
> ⁵_____, I need to get ready for work. I hope you like my idea about meeting. It's been ⁶_____ since we last saw each other!
>
> ⁷_____.
>
> Love,
> Harry

2 Read the Focus box. Then decide if sentences 1–5 below are true (T) or false (F).

Using informal words and expressions

When you write a personal email to someone you know well, you write as if you are speaking to the person directly. You use many of the same words and expressions that you use when you are having a conversation.

Starting a new statement using *so*
So, I just wanted to ask if you're doing anything …

Showing a change or contrast of topic using *anyway, by the way*
Anyway, let me know what you think.
It's not a really formal thing, by the way …

Asking direct questions
Are you still enjoying San Francisco?

Using short forms
How's life?
… they've asked me to come.

Using informal words and phrases
Hey Kate, how's it going?
I haven't been in touch for ages.
Do you fancy … ?
It would be awesome.

1 'So' is one way to start a sentence in an informal email. _____
2 'How's life?' is more informal than 'How is life?'. _____
3 'Are you doing anything this weekend?' is more informal than 'I would like to know if you are free this weekend'. _____
4 Using the word 'awesome' is a great way to change the topic. _____
5 When you write an informal email, write the way that you speak. _____

Prepare

3 **You're going to write an email to a friend giving them your news. Choose real situations or use the ideas below and make notes.**
- new house in the country (describe it)
- first dinner party in the new house last weekend (describe who came)
- tried a new recipe (describe the recipe)

Write

4 **Write your email using your notes in Exercise 3 and the Focus box to help you. Include language from Exercise 1.**

Vocabulary
Everyday activities

1 **Cross out the verb that does not go with the gadget or appliance.**
   1 *turn up / empty / load* a washing machine
   2 *switch on / unload / charge* a laptop
   3 *load / switch off / switch on* a light bulb
   4 *fill / turn up / turn down* an air conditioner
   5 *charge / switch on / empty* a mobile phone
   6 *unload / turn down / load* a dishwasher
   7 *unload / switch on / fill* a car
   8 *load / fill / switch on* a kettle

2 **Choose the correct alternatives.**

Saving energy is important. Using less energy can save you money and help the environment. But how can we do this?

Tip 1

When you leave your house, remember to switch ¹*on/off* electrical appliances and lights.

Tip 2

Everybody loves a cup of tea or coffee, but did you know that regularly ²*filling/loading* the kettle with more water than you need is one of the most expensive things you can do? ³*Loading/Unloading* the dishwasher too often is also another way to waste money.

Tip 3

People usually ⁴*empty/charge* their mobile phones and laptops all night, but this is a waste of electricity. These gadgets only need a few hours.

Tip 4

Turning ⁵*up/down* the heating is also another great way to save electricity. If you are cold, then put on a jumper instead of turning up the heat! In the summer, instead of switching ⁶*on/off* the air conditioner, buy a fan.

Tip 5

It's so normal for us to ⁷*switch on/charge* the TV when we're at home, but how often do we suddenly discover that no one is watching, or no one is even in the same room?

Follow our tips and you'll save money and electricity. Remember, be smart and switch it ⁸*off/on*!

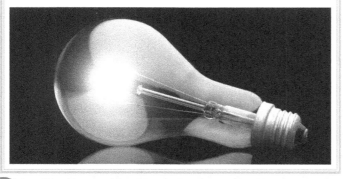

Grammar
Second conditional

3 **Match the sentence halves.**
   1 If they worked hard,
   2 If he left at nine,
   3 If I could help,
   4 If we didn't exercise and eat well,
   5 You would feel less stressed
   6 If we didn't have electricity,
   7 There would be less pollution
   8 If I could travel anywhere in the world,

   a if you didn't work so hard.
   b they could win the competition.
   c we would be unhealthy.
   d if people stopped using plastic bags.
   e I would.
   f life would be a lot harder.
   g I would go to Paris.
   h he could be there before lunch.

4 **Put the words in the correct order to make sentences. Use the comma to help you.**
   1 If / they would tell me / they knew,
     If they knew, they would tell me.
   2 I had more free time, / I would learn Japanese / If
     ....
   3 If / we would be healthier / we walked more,
     ....
   4 we would talk more / we didn't have mobile phones, / If
     ....
   5 he didn't have a car, / If / he wouldn't get to work on time
     ....

5 **Complete the questions with the correct form of the verbs in brackets. Use the second conditional.**
   1 What .... (change) if we .... (not have) mobile phones?
   2 What .... (happen) if the internet .... (go down)?
   3 If there .... (be) fewer cars on the roads, ... (it be) better for the environment?
   4 What .... (I do) if I .... (not live) in the city centre?

6 **Complete the sentences with the correct form of the verbs in brackets. Use the second conditional.**
   a Of course. If people .... (use) more public transport, there .... (be) less pollution.
   b If we .... (not spend) so much time on our phones, we .... (have) better conversations with our friends and family.
   c We .... (call) Dad and get it reconnected!
   d I don't know! If you .... (live) in the countryside, I'm sure you .... (not like) it.

7 **Match questions 1–4 in Exercise 5 with answers a–d in Exercise 6.**
   1 ....   2 ....   3 ....   4 ....

6B

Vocabulary

Describing bad behaviour and crime

1 Match the sentences halves.

1 Dropping ....
2 Jumping the ....
3 Speeding ....
4 Cheating ....
5 Lying about ....
6 Stealing things ....

a is against the law, and can cause accidents.
b in exams is wrong.
c your age is not illegal.
d litter on the streets is just rude.
e from your friends is really dishonest.
f queue is not fair to everyone else.

2 Complete the missing words.

1 He's always so late, it's just r_____e.
2 Is it against t_____e l_____w to smoke in restaurants here?
3 Driving without lights at night is i_____l.
4 It was really d_____t of her to say the gift was from her; it was from both of us.
5 Why are you giving him more of the cake? That's not f_____r!

Grammar

Structures for giving advice

3 Read the problems and choose the correct alternative.

1 Oh no! I can't find my wallet!
   a Don't worry. If I am you, I'd call the restaurant where we had lunch.
   b <u>Don't worry. If I were you, I'd call the restaurant where we had lunch.</u>

2 Mina is so stressed. Her boss sends her emails all the time, even when she's finished work!
   a She should talked to him and explain how she feels.
   b She should talk to him and tell him how she feels.

3 Joe is really angry and he isn't speaking to me. I don't know what to do.
   a You could call him and tell him that you are sorry.
   b You could to call him and tell him that you are sorry.

4 He's always saying stupid things to me during the lessons.
   a You ought to tell the teacher.
   b You ought tell the teacher.

5 We know that he stole the money, but what should we do about it?
   a If I were you, I would to tell the truth. It's the right thing to do.
   b If I were you, I would tell the truth. It's the right thing to do.

6 People who talk loudly on public transport really annoy me.
   a I know, but you shouldn't say anything. It's a public place!
   b I know, but you shouldn't to say anything. It's a public place.

7 I don't think I'll tell anyone about it.
   a If I were you, I would.
   b If I am you, I will.

8 I don't think I need to phone him, do I?
   a I think you ought phone him, yes.
   b I think you ought to phone him, yes.

4 Complete the conversation with the expressions in the box.

> I ought to   I think you should   If I were you   So what should
> What do you think I should do?   You shouldn't

A: Raquel left the office early again yesterday! This is the third time this week. I'm really annoyed. It's so unfair.

B: The third time this week! Wow, that's a lot. Does your boss know?

A: No, my boss is never there in the evenings, so she doesn't know. ¹_____

B: ²_____, I'd tell your boss. She should know if her employees leave work early.

A: Hm, I don't want to do that. It's quite serious and my boss is very busy at the moment.

B: Well, ³_____ say something to Raquel then. It's very dishonest to leave work early so often.

A: I agree. I'll speak to her tomorrow. ⁴_____ think about what I'm going to say!

B: ⁵_____ feel bad, Jake. It's the right thing to do.

A: You're right. ⁶_____ I say?

B: Er, that's your decision! Good luck!

Vocabulary
Environmental issues

1 **Match the sentence halves.**

1 Smoking can damage ___d___
2 We should use less plastic and help protect the _____
3 If there were fewer cars on the roads, it would reduce _____
4 Don't waste _____
5 Give money to wildlife organisations and help to support _____
6 Switch off appliances when you are not using them and help _____
7 Everybody should recycle old _____
8 Don't throw away products like _____

a their work.
b environment.
c clothes – give them to people who need them.
d your health.
e paper! Use the other side of it!
f save energy.
g glass, plastic and paper. Recycle them instead.
h air pollution.

2 **Complete the texts with the words in the boxes.**

recycle   reduce   save   throw away

> In the UK alone, we ¹_____ seven million tonnes of food and drink that we don't eat every year. That's a huge amount of food! We need to ²_____ the amount of food that we waste and think about ways to ³_____ the packaging and reuse the food that we don't need. When shopping, we should only buy as much food as we really need and ⁴_____ the food that we don't eat for later.
> It's time to do something! The environment needs you!

destroy   kill   protect   reuse

> Plastic is one of the biggest polluters. Plastic products in seas and oceans ⁵_____ fish, sea animals and birds and ⁶_____ the environment. It's time to stop buying plastic bottles and packaging and buy glass bottles that you can ⁷_____ instead. Small changes can make a difference and help to ⁸_____ the environment.
> It's time to do something! The environment needs you!

Grammar
Question tags

3 **Choose the correct alternative.**

1 You don't have much time today, *do/are* you?
2 I think you know Danny, *don't/haven't* you?
3 You're tired, *aren't/haven't* you?
4 She's been here before, *hasn't/isn't* she?
5 We're having the ice cream, and you'd like the cake, *wouldn't/don't* you?
6 It would be easier if we met later, wouldn't *we/it*?
7 I don't think she's so sure, *does she/is she*?
8 People can be so strange, can't *it/they*?
9 It won't work, *will/work* it?
10 He's coming tonight, *isn't/hasn't* he?
11 We all have to go, *have not/don't* we?
12 You think the same as I do, don't *I/you*?

4 **Complete the questions with question tags.**

1 You don't think we do enough to support organisations that protect the environment, _____*do you*_____?
2 We can all make a difference, _____?
3 Air pollution damages our health, _____?
4 We need to do more to protect the environment, _____?
5 It isn't right to destroy the places where animals live, _____?
6 There are too many cars on the roads nowadays, _____?
7 We can't throw away all of that food, _____?
8 There's too much plastic in the oceans and seas, _____?

Functional language
Make and respond to requests

1 Complete the conversation with the phrases in the box.

> afraid I can't do that   If it wouldn't be too much trouble
> It depends   sure, no problem   Would you mind

A: Hello Peter, Tim here.

B: Oh, hi Tim. How are you?

A: Good, I'm actually calling to ask for a favour. I'm moving house next Saturday, you see.

B: Really? How exciting. It's quite a busy time, isn't it?

A: Yes, there's so much to do. **1** _____ helping me? I have so many boxes!

B: On Saturday? I'm **2** _____ . I have plans with my family. It's my niece's birthday.

A: Oh right. Well, what about Sunday then?

B: Sunday? Yes, **3** _____ . I'm free all day. Would you like me to ask Mark if he can help, too?

A: Yes, please! That would be great.

B: Can I do anything else for you?

A: Well actually, I did have another favour. But I'm not sure you'll agree to it!

B: Hm? **4** _____ what it is.

A: **5** _____ would you be able to look after my cats?

B: Tim, you know the answer will be no. I hate cats!

A: I understand. It's a lot to ask. What about the dog?

2 Put the conversation in the correct order.

a Hey Misato. What do you need this time? _____

b Sure, no problem, I can lend you that. I thought you were going to ask for something big. _____

c Ha-ha, yes I know, I'm always asking for things. Yes, well, do you think you could do me a big favour? _____

d Thank you so much ... Now, the second favour is a bit bigger ... _____

e The second favour? You didn't say there were two! _____

f Hey John, you're looking well. _1_

g I knew it. Go on, what is it? _____

h Would it be possible for you to lend me $100 until pay day? _____

i Yes, sorry, I forgot to mention that there were two. So ... Would it be possible for me to stay with you for two nights next week? The landlord needs to do something to my place ... _____

j Oh yes, I remember, you told me. OK, no problem, I'll ask somebody else. _____

k Sorry, I'm afraid I can't help you with that one. My sister is staying with me next week. _____

Listening

1 🔊 6.01 **Listen to an expert on home safety and put the following items in the order that you hear them.**

a bedside lamp _____

b shower mat _____

c shoes _____

d dishwasher _____

e gas _____

2 Listen again. Are the sentences true (T) or false (F)?

1 The presenter seriously hurt himself in the shower. _____

2 Sharon recommends having something in the shower so you don't slip. _____

3 Sharon says these accidents never end in death. _____

4 Sharon suggests unloading the dishwasher when it's finished. _____

5 No one has gas these days, so we don't need to worry about this problem. _____

6 Sharon describes falling over a chair in the bedroom. _____

7 Sharon says you may have an accident if you get up in the night when you're sleepy. _____

3 Listen again and choose the best summary of Sharon's talk.

a Accidents don't happen very often at home, but we should take care when it's dark or when the bathroom is wet.

b Accidents can happen anywhere in the home. You can avoid them by being organised and tidy, and knowing what the possible dangers are.

c The most important thing is to make sure you have the safest appliances. You need to pay extra for these, but it's worth it because your safety is the most important thing.

Reading

1 Read the problem page and match problems 1–3 with advice a–c below.

1 I'm a parent of three children and there are some girls in my daughter's class who **bully** her on social media. She uses her phone a lot and was starting to behave strangely. I decided to look at her phone and I found some very **cruel** messages. I recognised one of the girls as she used to come and play when my daughter was younger. I also know her mum very well because we go to yoga together. In fact, I'll see her tomorrow. I'm so angry I want to say something to the mother, but I have to be careful and protect my daughter from more bullying. ....

2 I think my partner is shoplifting! The last time we went shopping, I saw her take something off the shelf and put it in her bag. I couldn't believe it at first because we have a comfortable life. It all started when she lost her job two years ago and she started taking small things like sugar. We used to joke about it, but I never thought it was serious. The latest shoplifting **incident** has started to make me think that maybe she has a problem. ....

3 I have a friend who's always borrowing things from me. I normally don't mind, but the last time she borrowed an expensive fan. When she returned it to me, I turned it on and it didn't work. I have no real proof that she broke it, but I know that it was working perfectly when I last used it. I feel very uncomfortable telling her, but it was an expensive fan. I really don't want to lend her anything else and I'm worried about what I'm going to say the next time she asks. ....

2 Read the problem page again and answer the questions.

1 How did the parent in problem 1 find out about the bullying?

....

....

2 When did the person in problem 2 notice there was a problem?

....

....

3 How does the person in problem 3 feel about lending her friend anything else?

....

....

4 In Deidre's opinion, why do some people steal?

....

....

5 What is Deidre's advice in problem 3?

....

....

3 Match words 1–5 with definitions or synonyms a–e.

1 bully ....
2 cruel ....
3 incident ....
4 thrill ....
5 the sooner the better ....

a something that happens, often something bad
b strong feeling of excitement
c very quickly
d enjoying doing bad things to people
e to scare or frighten someone

a I'm afraid what she's doing is illegal and you're lucky she wasn't caught. You should speak to her and I would say, **the sooner the better** before she gets into trouble. Normally there's a psychological reason for stealing and it can be addictive. Some people enjoy the **thrill** of it. Anyway, you need to find the cause and resolve it ASAP.

b I'm sorry your daughter is having problems with bullying. As a mother, I can imagine how angry you must be feeling, but you should speak to the school before you speak to anyone else. Is there someone you can tell? Before you make any contact, if I were you, I would speak to your daughter.

c If this is a true friend, then you should be able to speak to her openly. It's unfair to abuse your generosity and if you don't tell her now, this behaviour will continue. I would just tell her politely that you noticed that it was broken. Her reaction will tell you everything you need to know.

6

Writing

1 Look at opinions 1–5 and tick (✓) the ones which suggest that individuals can help to protect the environment.

1 Many people say that the environment is too badly damaged and it's too late for the individual to help. ....

2 If we, the people, don't do anything, there could be serious consequences for our planet. ....

3 Governments must take more responsibility for the environment. ....

4 Individuals don't have the time and money to make a difference. ....

5 Small acts can make a big difference if we all help. ....

2 Complete the essay with the phrases in the box.

However   In addition (x2)   In conclusion
Many people think that   On the other hand
There are different views on this subject

Can we make a difference?

A Today there is so much news about environmental problems and discussion about what we should do about them. So, as individuals, how much can we do to help? Do small acts make a difference? **1** ....

B **2** .... we can do a lot on a day-to-day basis. Saving more energy at home by turning appliances and other machines off can make a big difference to the energy we use. This is easy to do and if we all did it every day, we would notice a change. **3** .... , our food choices have an effect on the environment, from eating meat to the packaging that food comes in. By eating less meat and more vegetables, we can help reduce environmental damage.

C **4** .... , some say it's simply too late. Global warming and climate change show us the impact of our past behaviour. These people believe that governments need to do more. This means having more laws to control pollution and farming. **5** .... , people say that the government needs to improve all systems in industry and agriculture.

D **6** .... , people have different opinions about how much individuals can do. **7** .... , we can all do something, whether it's something big or small.

3 Read the Focus box and match paragraphs A–D with functions 1–4 below.

Organising ideas

In a for and against essay, you give reasons and information to support different opinions about a topic. You want to help the reader understand the issues and decide for themselves who or what is right or wrong.

Introduction: In your introduction, state the topic for discussion.

Middle paragraphs: In one paragraph, give reasons and information **in support of** the topic. In another paragraph, give reasons and information **against** the topic.

It's important not to support one opinion or the other in the two main paragraphs. Use phrases like this:
Some/Many people say/think …
Other people disagree/believe …

Conclusion: In your conclusion, you can repeat the main points and say what you personally think or make a recommendation.

Paragraph A ....
Paragraph B ....
Paragraph C ....
Paragraph D ....

1 Reasons and information in support of the topic
2 Conclusion with the main points and your personal opinion and a recommendation
3 Introduction stating the topic for discussion
4 Reasons and information against the topic

Prepare

4 You are going to write an essay. Choose a topic from the list below or think of your own. Make notes for each paragraph and think of some for and against arguments.

• People living in flats should not have animals.
• We need higher taxes for car owners to reduce pollution.
• Recycling is a waste of time.

Write

5 Write your essay. Use your notes in Exercise 4 and the Focus box to help you.

Vocabulary

Skills and abilities

1 Cross out the incorrect alternative.

This programme is designed to help you ¹*gain*/*create*/*develop* excellent communication skills so you are more confident when dealing with clients. You will ²*prepare*/*work on*/*gain* presentations to give other members of the group and ³*work on*/*develop*/*gain* new friendships which will help you expand your clientele and work opportunities.

Want to write but don't know where to start? This writing course is for you! We ask all applicants to ⁴*develop*/*gain*/*write* a short story and upload it onto our website. Successful candidates will be invited onto our new course where you will ⁵*get*/*improve*/*gain* an official writing qualification.

Tired of asking your colleagues for help when you have a computer problem? We offer a course in basic computer skills which will help you to ⁶*gain*/*change*/*increase your* confidence with computers. We also offer more advanced classes for people who are interested in ⁷*uploading*/*designing*/ *creating* their own website.

2 Complete the conversations with the correct form of the words in the box.

> edit   design   gain   improve (x2)   learn   prepare   take

1 **A:** Hey Kate. How's your daughter enjoying the course?
   B: Oh, she loves it. Last week, she learnt how to ¹_____ her own website, and next week she's doing a course on how to take and ²_____ photos.

2 **A:** Hi John. How was Thailand?
   B: Oh, superb. I think the best bit though was the cooking course. I learnt how to ³_____ an authentic green curry.
   A: Oh, fabulous, will you teach me?
   B: Of course! In fact, I still want to ⁴_____ my cooking skills.

3 **A:** Hi Sue. Have you started your painting course yet?
   B: Yes, I have. It's only been two weeks, but I think I'm starting to ⁵_____ some confidence.
   A: That's great. I'd love to ⁶_____ a course like that. I used to paint when I was younger, but I'd like to ⁷_____ my technique.

4 **A:** Mel says she's going to ⁸_____ how to ride a horse.
   B: Wow! I hope she doesn't fall off!

Grammar

Modal verbs: ability

3 Choose the correct alternatives.

1 *Could you*/*You were able* draw when you were younger?

2 *Were you able*/*Can you* to put up the shelves this morning or shall I do it?

3 I *wasn't able*/*couldn't* come to class because I was working late.

4 At the end of this course, I'll *be able to*/ *won't be able* design my own website.

5 I *can't*/*am able* write fiction very well, but I'm good at editing.

6 He *won't be able*/*can't* to lift this. It's too heavy.

4 Rewrite the sentences so that they mean the same. Use *can*, *could* or *be able to* in the correct form.

1 She is a great dancer.
   She _____can dance_____ very well.

2 It was impossible for me to learn the dance moves.
   I _____ the dance moves.

3 There's a possibility that she could sell some paintings if she wins the art competition.
   She will be _____ sell some paintings if she wins the art competition.

4 At first, I couldn't edit my photos, but now I can.
   Now I'm _____ edit my photos.

5 If you're unable to find the exact ingredients, you can use substitutes.
   If you _____ the exact ingredients, you can use substitutes.

6 I used to speak a little French, but I don't think I can remember anything now.
   I _____ speak French any more.

7 I tried to speak to Tim, but he wasn't there.
   I _____ speak to Tim because he wasn't there.

8 In the end, I got into my flat by climbing the wall.
   I _____ get into my flat by climbing the wall.

Vocabulary

Milestones

1 Match verbs 1–8 with words a–h.

1	fall	a	your job
2	win	b	house
3	get	c	a driving test
4	lose	d	travelling
5	move	e	university
6	go	f	in love
7	finish	g	married
8	pass	h	an award

2 Complete the letter with the words in the box.

> fallen   find   gone   got   lost   moved
> passed   win

Dear Pat,

I'm sorry I haven't been in touch for so long – we've had a busy year! The children have finally left home and it's very quiet in the house, I must say. Dan has ¹_____ travelling. He's starting in Europe and then plans to go to North Africa. Debbie has just started her company as a life coach and is doing very well. Life has been very busy for her this year. She finally ²_____ married to John in the summer and last month they ³_____ house. It's a beautiful cottage not far from me. Unfortunately, Pete ⁴_____ his job last year and has been in and out of work ever since. He's thinking of retraining as an electrician, so we hope he'll start his course in the New Year. I'm sure he'll ⁵_____ a better job. On a positive note, he thinks he's ⁶_____ in love with a Swedish girl ... wonderful because I would quite like to visit Sweden! He has also just ⁷_____ his driving test!

We're all healthy, which is the most important thing, and we're still hoping to ⁸_____ the lottery one day!

Write and tell me all your news.

Love,
Sandra

Grammar

Past perfect

3 Put the words in the correct order to make sentences.

1 I arrived at / the station / the train / When / had left
_____

2 I moved / before / I'd / finished university / to Spain
_____

3 By / he'd / lost five jobs / the time / he turned 20
_____

4 After / I went / travelled through Europe, / to Africa / I'd
_____

5 an actress / to be / always wanted / I'd
_____

6 after / I / didn't know / I'd left school / what to do
_____

4 Complete the sentences with the words in the box.

> after (x2)   already   before   by (x2)

1 _____ he had left, she realised she really loved him.
2 When they arrived, she'd _____ gone.
3 _____ the time she was 15, she'd won three awards.
4 _____ they had finished the project, they went out to celebrate.
5 She'd seen him _____ he saw her, then crossed the road to avoid him.
6 He had made a lot of money _____ the time he was 21.

5 Correct the mistake in each sentence.

1 Pete ~~had~~ lost his job last month, so he's looking for a new one.

2 I had just decided to take the new job when my boss had asked me to stay.

3 Before Anya learnt to drive, her dad has already bought her a new car.

4 By the time he was 18, Chris already left home.

5 She had already won the lottery twice after she won a million euros last month.

6 Kirsten lived in the house for a long time when she decided to sell it.

7 When they got married, they've already known each other for ten years.

Vocabulary

Outdoor equipment

1 **Complete the missing words in the definitions.**

1 A b_____ is a large bag you carry on your back.
2 A waterproof j_____ is an item of clothing which protects you from the rain.
3 Walking b_____ are special shoes for hiking.
4 A camping s_____ is for cooking when you go camping.
5 Insect r_____ protects you from insect bites.
6 A portable c_____ fills your phone or tablet battery with electricity.

2 **Complete the text with the words in the box. There are three extra words.**

> backpack   camping stove   insect repellent   portable charger
> sunglasses   sunscreen   tent   torch   walking boots
> waterproof jacket

My first music festival was awesome! I think it was the best weekend of my life, although it wasn't all perfect! I'd bought a new
¹ _____ – it was bigger than I thought and I was worried it was too big for the car! It was forecast to be sunny and warm, so I packed my ² _____ and ³ _____ .
We got to the campsite at lunchtime. By the time we'd unpacked, we were all so hungry, but luckily Sandra had brought a
⁴ _____ , so we could cook! That was good fun. Oh, but I almost forgot the first disaster – so, when we were all unpacking Trish realised she hadn't brought her ⁵ _____ and so her phone died. Oh, and then Mike was attacked by mosquitoes, but of course, Sandra was prepared with her ⁶ _____ .
The bands were all incredible – I haven't danced so much in my life! My mum had given me a ⁷ _____ , so luckily we could find our way around in the dark! On the last day it rained heavily, but then a festival wouldn't be a festival without rain!

3 **Complete the sentences with the words in the box.**

> insect repellent   portable charger   sleeping bag   sunglasses
> sunscreen   tent   ~~torch~~   waterproof jacket

1 It's something you use to see in the dark.   _torch_
2 You put this on your skin so you don't burn when it's hot.
   _____
3 You wear this when it rains.   _____
4 You use this to protect yourself from mosquitoes.   _____
5 You use this for keeping warm at night.   _____
6 You wear these to protect you from bright light.   _____
7 Take one of these so that your phone doesn't die.   _____
8 If you go camping, you and your friends can sleep in one of these.
   _____

Grammar

Expressing purpose

4 **Choose the correct alternatives.**

1 Take a coat *so/that* you don't get cold.
2 This is really good repellent *for/to* keeping the mosquitoes away.
3 Take this torch with you *so that/for* you can find the path at night. There are no street lights there.
4 Take your phone *so that/for* you don't get lost.
5 I'm going to the US *to/so that* visit the Grand Canyon.
6 There are special areas *to/for* put your bags in.
7 You'll need to complete a form *to/so that* open an account.
8 Have you got anything *for/to* opening bottles?

5 **Match the sentence halves.**

① Bring some good walking boots   _____
② Please be punctual   _____
③ There will be a phone signal on most parts of the walk   _____
④ We must drink water   _____
⑤ We'll stop   _____
⑥ We recommend an insect repellent   _____
⑦ It's a difficult hike   _____
⑧ Please see the map attached   _____

ⓐ so you will be able to contact us in case of emergency.
ⓑ to have lunch at 3 p.m.
ⓒ so that we can leave on time.
ⓓ for keeping the mosquitos away!
ⓔ so if you have any health issues, it's probably not suitable.
ⓕ so that you feel comfortable while you're walking.
ⓖ in order to stay hydrated.
ⓗ so that you can become familiar with the area.

Functional language

Ask for information

1 Put the words in the correct order to make questions.

1 anything else / I can / for you / do / Is there?

No, thanks very much for your help.

2 you / help / Can / I?

Yes, I'm interested in studying Spanish and would like to find out more about the classes you offer.

3 what time / Can you tell me / they / start?

Yes, at two o'clock.

4 English classes / offer / Do you?

We don't sorry, only French and German.

5 some information about / what courses / Can you / give me / you offer?

Of course, what type of course are you interested in?

6 say / Could you / again / that?

Yes, we close at 9 p.m. Monday to Friday.

7 sending me / Would you / mind / a brochure?

Certainly, you should have it before Friday.

8 if you / could / I wonder / give me / some advice?

Sure, have a seat!

2 Complete the conversation with the phrases in the box.

> got that   can I   you mind   interested in   calling to
> could you

A: Hello, I'm ¹_____ find out about your French classes.

B: Yes, how ²_____ help?

A: ³_____ tell me how much the classes cost?

B: They're £25 for an hour for group classes and £45 for private classes.

A: OK, ⁴_____ , thank you. Also, I'm ⁵_____ doing your Advanced Diploma, is that possible?

B: Yes, we offer every level, including the Advanced Diploma.

A: Right. Would ⁶_____ sending me your brochure?

B: Not at all. If you give me your address, I'll send it out to you today.

Listening

1 🔊 7.01 Listen to three people talking about trips they've taken. Match speakers 1–3 with photos A–C.

1 Sarah ____   2 Jude ____   3 Georgina ____

2 Listen again and complete the table with the correct information.

	Where did they go?	Why?
Sarah		
Jude		
Georgina		

3 Listen again and complete the sentences.

1 Sarah's husband organised a surprise for their _____ wedding anniversary.

2 On the morning they were leaving, Sarah's husband gave her a _____ and some _____ .

3 Sarah had travelled through _____ before but not South America.

4 Jude went on her trip when she had finished _____ .

5 Jude doesn't want to go back to Paris because _____ .

6 Georgina was _____ when she went on her first camping trip with her family.

7 At night Georgina and her brothers told _____ in their tent, using torches.

Reading

1 Write three things you could do to reduce stress.

1 ....

2 ....

3 ....

2 Read the text. Does it mention your ideas?

3 Read the text again and answer the questions.

1 What did Martin do to try and deal with stress?

....

....

2 What does Martin make sure he does every day?

....

....

3 When did Maggie start designing clothes?

....

4 Why did Maggie quit her office job?

....

....

5 Why did Dave go on holiday?

....

6 Where did he go?

....

....

7 Why should you try to get away from the office?

....

....

4 Match the words in bold in the text with meanings 1–5.

1 saying funny things

....

2 a need for a product to be made or sold

....

3 relax and forget about pressures such as work

....

4 organise something, e.g. a holiday or an appointment

....

5 the answer to a problem

....

Three ways to de-stress and be happier

Studies show that nine out of ten people feel like they don't have enough time to slow down and relax. Stress levels are higher than ever before. So how do you deal with stress? Read on to discover ways to manage and reduce your stress levels and live a healthier life.

1 Laugh more

With the day-to-day pressures of work, study and family, it can be hard to remember to slow down and enjoy all the good things in our lives. The healthy things. The *funny* things. Laughter has been found to decrease levels of stress and increase the production of chemicals that make us feel good.

Martin (28) from London tells us about his experience.

'When I'd finished university, I felt like I just didn't stop, there was always something to do – pass my driving test, get a good job, get married, have children. I became so focused on the things that I had to do that I forgot to smile and laugh and enjoy my time with friends. Last year, I decided to take more time for myself. Now, whether it's watching a funny film or **joking** with friends, I make sure I take time to laugh every day and I've never felt better!'

2 Take a course or learn a new skill

Studies show that taking time to take a new course, gain a qualification or develop new skills is one of the best ways to beat stress and help us to feel calm and relaxed. For example you could sign up for an evening class to learn how to cook or make furniture, or if you'd rather stay at home you could do a course online.

Maggie (43) from Cambridge tells us how she did it.

'About five years ago, I started designing clothes for my friends. I had a really busy job in an office and creating my own clothes at the weekends really helped me relax. I created my own website and suddenly everybody wanted to buy my clothes! I had to quit my office job so that I could meet the **demand** and continue to make clothes. Now I do what I love every day. It's stressful, but it's good stress because I'm doing what I love!'

3 Take a break from work

Going on holiday is not just enjoyable, but it's also necessary for good health and reducing stress levels. Many of us spend more hours than we should sitting in offices, and just a little break can make a difference. A holiday will give you something to look forward to and you'll work better when you get back to the office.

Dave (38) from Melbourne says,

'I felt like I couldn't stop thinking about work. I wasn't able to switch off, even at the weekends. I knew I needed to do something different and a wildlife safari in South Africa was the **solution**.'

Whether you have the time and the money to go on a long trip like Dave or simply go on a camping trip nearer home, you should try to get away from the office – even for 24 hours – because it's been shown to reduce stress and increase levels of happiness. So go ahead, **book** your holiday today!

Writing

1 Read the leaflet and match headings a–e with paragraphs 1–5.

   a Contact us
   b What can you do to help?
   c When will the guided tours take place?
   d Who are we?
   e Why are we doing this?

Want to find out about our town's history? Come and join us this Saturday from 9 a.m. to 9 p.m.

1

We're a group of local businesses and people who are passionate about our town. We believe that the story of this historic town should be told to everybody and what better way to do this than through guided tours with local historians.

2

This town has a lot of stories to tell and a rich and interesting historical past. This is a great opportunity to see the town as you've never seen it before – we guarantee that you'll be surprised! Money from the tours will be used to help protect and conserve local landmarks, such as the castle, the town centre and the clock tower.

3

Tours will start at 9 a.m. in the morning and will last approximately two hours. The last tour will begin at 9 p.m. and includes the haunted areas of the town. Perfect for those of you interested in ghosts!

4

Tours cost £5 per person and all money from the tours goes towards protecting the old buildings and monuments in our town. So please come and support us and bring your family and friends!

5

For more information call Laura or visit our website and sign up today!

2 Read the Focus box and find examples of imperatives and positive adjectives in the leaflet in Exercise 1.

Engaging a reader

When we create a leaflet, we should think of how we can make people interested in what we are telling them about. There are a few ways we can do this:

Asking questions
Want to find out about our town's history?
What can you do to help?

Using imperatives
Come and **support** us and **bring** your family and friends!

Using positive adjectives
*This town has a lot of stories to tell and a **rich** and **interesting** historical past.*

3 Choose the more engaging alternative, A or B.

  1 **A** If you are bored at the weekend, you can come and join us.
       B Bored at the weekend? Come and join us!

  2 **A** We offer seafood dishes from the Blue Coast.
       B We offer amazing seafood dishes from the beautiful Blue Coast.

  3 **A** Start the year with a fresh new look.
       B You can begin the year with a new look.

  4 **A** It's very frustrating waiting in traffic, so it's a good idea to cycle instead.
       B Tired of sitting in traffic? Why don't you jump on your bike?

  5 **A** It's a new cafe which offers Brazilian coffee.
       B It's an exciting new café which offers delicious Brazilian coffee.

  6 **A** Do you want to do something new? Call us today!
       B If you want to try something new, then you can call us and talk to us about it.

Prepare

4 You're going to write the information leaflet for an event in your local area. Make notes using the questions below.

- What type of event are you planning?
- Who is organising the event?
- Why are you organising the event?
- What kind of activities will you offer?
- What will the event/activities help people do?
- What do you want people who read the leaflet to do?
- How can they contact you?

5 Plan your leaflet. Think of questions, imperatives and adjectives that you can include.

Write

6 Write your information leaflet. Use your notes in Exercise 4 and the language in Exercise 5 to help you.

Vocabulary
Multi-word verbs

1 Choose the correct alternatives.

1 Don't forget to clear *back/up* the classroom at the end of the day.
2 Students must hand *in/on* their homework at the beginning of each lesson.
3 Please remember to take *down/out* the rubbish.
4 Everyone must join *on/in* all class activities.
5 Put *away/off* all books in your lockers before you leave.
6 If he doesn't deal *with/on* the problem, I will.
7 Hi Joe. Call me *back/off* when you have time.
8 How many times do I need to tell you? Shut *down/up* your computer before you leave the office!

2 Complete sentences A and B with the same phrasal verb.

1 A He shuts ___*down*___ the machines at 5 p.m. and takes a break.
 B My laptop sometimes shuts ___*down*___ by itself.
2 A Why don't you throw _____ your old clothes? You never wear them.
 B Don't throw _____ that food. I'll eat it.
3 A If you borrow something from my desk, please put it _____ .
 B I took the umbrella from the hall, but I forgot to put it _____ .
4 A Everyone was dancing but Tina didn't join _____ .
 B Don't be shy, join _____ the activity with everyone else.
5 A It's your turn to take _____ the rubbish. Can you do it now?
 B The dentist had to take _____ her tooth. It was very painful.
6 A It's a good job, but I don't like dealing _____ all the paperwork.
 B Dealing _____ difficult situations is part of my job.

Grammar
Modal verbs: obligation and necessity

3 Read the sentences and tick (✓) the sentences where there is an obligation.

1 You must look after your belongings. ✓
2 You don't have to wear a uniform.
3 You have to clear up your room.
4 She didn't need to worry.
5 You mustn't speak Spanish in class.
6 You must be 17 to get a driving licence in the UK.
7 She doesn't need a visa to travel here.

4 Complete the text with the words in the box. The words can be used more than once.

> allowed must need

Hi Jo,
I really hope you enjoy staying in our flat this weekend. While you're in our beautiful city, you really **1** _____ visit the Reina Sofia museum, and relax in the Retiro park for an hour or two. You don't **2** _____ to walk far to get from one to the other, so that could be a nice day out for you.
Just some notes about the flat. We're not **3** _____ to smoke in there, but if I remember correctly, you don't smoke. If you **4** _____ to cook, remember that you **5** _____ to turn on the gas at the bottle first.
There's some food in the cupboards, so please use whatever you want, and you don't **6** _____ to worry about replacing it. You can take us out for an expensive dinner when we next meet! Oh, speaking of that, we **7** _____ try and meet up soon. It's been too long.
Anyway, have a great weekend!
Selina x

5 Rewrite the sentences using the words in brackets so that they have a similar meaning.

1 It's not necessary to come home early.
 You ___*don't have to*___ come home early. (have)
2 It's not necessary for students to wear a uniform on Fridays.
 Students _____ wear a uniform on Fridays. (need)
3 We could go to bed late in the summer!
 We _____ go to bed late in the summer! (allowed)
4 It was necessary to help in the house.
 We _____ help in the house. (had)
5 You can't smoke in this area.
 You _____ smoke in this area. (must)

Vocabulary

Comment adverbs

1 Choose the correct alternatives.

1 We were caught in a snow storm. *Thankfully/Sadly*, we were rescued.

2 *Unfortunately/Amazingly*, she started competing only a few months after her accident.

3 *Hopefully/Strangely*, there will be good sporting facilities for disabled young people.

4 *Luckily/Obviously*, we need to invest in better equipment.

5 He's considered one of the greatest actors of all time, but *strangely/hopefully*, he only started acting in films when he was 50!

6 *Luckily/Unfortunately*, we have to cancel the sports day due to bad weather conditions.

7 My mum fell. *Obviously/Luckily*, she wasn't badly injured.

8 John Lennon was a peace activist, songwriter and musician. *Tragically/Amazingly*, he was killed when he was only 40.

2 Complete the missing adverbs in the story.

Jane was an aspiring athlete and had big hopes to compete in the Olympics. After falling off a horse, Jane was ¹tr_____ly left paralysed and in a wheelchair. ²S_____ly, she had to say goodbye to her dreams of becoming a world class athlete. That didn't stop Jane. ³Am_____ly, she made very quick progress and decided she didn't want to stop competing. 'I had to think about taking up a new sport where I could compete, so I chose basketball because I had always liked watching it on the TV'. ⁴Lu_____ly, there was a club for reduced ability athletes in her community. Jane joined and became one of the best members in the team! After a few months, she travelled to France to compete in a competition. ⁵U_____ly, Jane's team lost, but that didn't stop her. 'If anything it made me want to win more!' Now Jane is practising for another European competition in Belgium. '⁶Ho_____ly, we will play well and take a cup home this time!'

Grammar

The passive: present and past

3 Match the sentence halves.

1 False legs are _____
2 He was _____
3 The children _____
4 Children with learning difficulties are _____
5 At that time, technology wasn't being _____
6 A group of skiers _____
7 We aren't _____
8 Tragically, one of the members was _____

a killed in the expedition.

b were found by a rescue team after they got lost on a school trip.

c allowed to take photos of the exhibition.

d considered one of the best climbers in the community.

e designed using the latest technology, and are much more comfortable than before.

f being given more opportunities today.

g used in the same way it is today.

h were caught in a snowstorm in the Alps.

4 Choose the correct alternatives.

1 A group of school children *was/be* injured in a coach accident.

2 More and more technology *is being/being* used in false legs these days.

3 Ten mountaineers *were rescued/are rescued* by locals in Alaska last week.

4 A woman was *found/find* a month after disappearing.

5 A French man *has given/was given* an award after rescuing two swimmers last year.

6 A child has been taken to hospital where she is *being/been* treated for rare insect bites.

5 Rewrite the active sentences in the passive form. Use *by* when necessary.

1 The rescue team found the lost hikers.
The hikers *were found by the rescue team* _____.

2 Experts are testing new equipment.
New equipment _____.

3 Scientists discovered a treatment for back injuries.
A new treatment for back injuries _____.

4 We are holding the games in Moscow.
The games _____.

5 No one was using the room when we arrived.
The room _____.

6 UNESCO made the Lake District a World Heritage site in 2017.
The Lake District _____.

Vocabulary

Geographical features

1 Choose the correct alternatives.

> This is a country of contrasts, so you will need at least two weeks to explore it. The first thing you will see as you land is the **1** *snow-covered/sandy* mountains. It's a good idea to hire a guide who can take you into these **2** *thick/rocky* mountains. While you're there, you will see **3** *high/deep* waterfalls which will take your breath away. Make sure you swim in the **4** *thick/clear* lakes and rivers – they are so clean you can see the bottom. At the foot of the mountains there are lots of small villages to visit and **5** *steep/clear* hills to climb! Only 20 miles from the mountains you have miles of beautiful **6** *thick/sandy* beaches.

2 Choose the correct alternatives.
1. Everest and K2 are the highest *mountains/hills* in the world.
2. The Nile and Mississippi are both *seas/rivers*.
3. The Rocky *Mountains/Cliffs* are in Canada, New Mexico and the US.
4. Madhya Pradesh is a thick *forest/beach* in India.
5. You can go boating on the *lake/valley* in good weather.
6. If you want sandy *beaches/waterfalls*, go to the Bahamas!
7. Is the area you live in quite flat or are there lots of *lakes/hills*?
8. I've always wanted to go to the Amazon *rainforest/peak*.
9. The most famous *waterfall/bay* is at Niagara. It's amazing to see all that water rushing down.
10. The town is at the bottom of this deep *coast/valley*, so you can't see it from here.
11. Don't go too near the edge of the *cliff/desert*, Tobias!
12. We reached the *peak/shore* of the mountain by 2 p.m.

Grammar

Non-defining relative clauses

3 Complete the description with the pronouns in the box below. The pronouns can be used more than once.

when	where	which	who	whose

The Lake District is a region in the north of England, **1** _____ you will find lakes, forests and mountains. It became an official place of natural beauty in 2017, **2** _____ it was made a UNESCO World Heritage site. William Wordsworth, **3** _____ was a romantic poet in the 1800s, wrote about the lakes in his literature. Today it is a very popular holiday destination, **4** _____ visitors can do many outdoor activities in beautiful surroundings. Kendal, **5** _____ is situated in the south of the region, is a pretty market town and worth visiting. Tour guides, **6** _____ speak various languages and **7** _____ knowledge of the region is excellent, can be booked through the local tourist board. The best time to visit is in the spring and summer, **8** _____ the weather is warm and you can enjoy all this region has to offer.

4 Combine the sentences.
1. The ancient mountain gives you the best view of the surroundings. It's 2,000 metres high.
   The ancient mountain, which is 2,000 metres high, gives you the best view of the surroundings.
2. The national park is in the north of England. You can see lots of wildlife there.
   _____
3. The best time to visit Seville is April. It's not too hot.
   _____
4. Here you find the most famous lakes. You'll never forget their beauty.
   _____
5. The Awa tribe are approximately 200 years old. They live in the Amazon.
   _____

Functional language
Make excuses and apologise

1 Match situations 1–4 with phrases a–d.

1 You're late for a dinner date with your friend. ....
2 Your friend forgot your birthday. ....
3 You haven't sent an important email to your boss. ....
4 You borrowed your friend's book and it had a small accident. ....

a 'Never mind. These things happen. I'm always forgetting dates!'
b 'I'm really sorry ... my boss asked me to do a report at the last minute. I came as fast as I could.'
c 'It was very stupid of me, but I put it in the washing machine by mistake.'
d 'I'm really sorry. I meant to do it before lunch, but I forgot. I'll do it right now.'

2 Choose the correct alternatives.

A: Dave. Have you finished the report yet? I'm meeting our new client tomorrow morning.

B: No, I'm ¹*really/true* sorry, but I've been so busy I haven't had time. I ²*had/must* to speak to lots of different clients this morning.

A: OK, but that's ³*no/none* excuse and you promised to finish it by the end of the day yesterday. We should really send it today.

B: Well, you ⁴*look/see*, I won't have time now. It's my son's birthday and we have a party at home. I can't stay any longer.

A: OK, ⁵*never mind/not mind*. I'll do it this time, but please don't let it happen again.

B: Of course not. Thanks, Rick.

3 Put the conversation in the correct order.

a **Charles:** Hey Josh, how's it going? ___1___
b **Josh:** I know, it was really stupid of me. Look I'm so sorry, I've been so busy recently. ....
c **Charles:** OK, look, never mind ... I've got another one I can use. ....
d **Josh:** Yeah, good thanks. What about you? ....
e **Charles:** Not too bad ... Listen, did you bring my suit in today? ....
f **Josh:** Yes, I know it's a bad excuse, OK? I meant to bring it today and I forgot. I'll go home and get it now. ....
g **Charles:** That's no excuse! We're all busy, Josh and I reminded you three times yesterday! ....
h **Josh:** Charles, look I'm really sorry, but I forgot. ....
i **Charles:** I need it, Josh! I've got an interview tomorrow morning! ....
j **Josh:** OK, if you're sure? I'll bring it tomorrow I promise. ....

Listening

1 🔊 **8.01** Listen to the radio programme. Are the statements true (T) or false (F)?

1 Human Achievement Day only celebrates the things that you have done in your own life. ....
2 The radio programme will include stories from people who listen to it. ....

2a Listen to Karen again and answer the questions.

1 Where did Karen's grandfather travel?
....
2 How many times did he climb Mount Everest?
....
3 What happened to his friend in France?
....
4 How long did it take them to get back down the mountain?
....

b Listen to Marta again. Are the sentences true (T) or false (F)?

1 Marta's friend was in a bad accident. ....
2 She was in hospital for less than six months. ....
3 Laura had plenty of free time, so it was easy for her to visit Marta. ....
4 Laura and Marta are going to do a sports event together. ....

c Listen to Sam again and choose the correct answers to the questions.

1 What does Sam think about his living situation?
  a He's very happy where he is.
  b He's not very happy and wants to move out.
2 How much work does Sam do around the house?
  a Very little – his mum does everything.
  b He does all the cooking and cleaning.
3 What do Sam's friends think about it?
  a They think he should stay.
  b They think he should leave.

Reading

1 Read the brochure and match headings a–e with paragraphs 1–5.

a Activities in natural areas ....

b Places of interest ....

c Travel and learn! ....

d Your new home ....

e Study details ....

2 Read the brochure again. Choose the correct alternatives to answer the questions.

1 Can the classes help students prepare for tests?

   a yes   b no   c it doesn't say

2 How long are English classes?

   a one hour

   b two hours with a break

   c four hours

3 How many types of outdoor activities do students do every week?

   a three   b five   c seven

4 What does the brochure say about the weather in England?

   a It rains all year.

   b It rains a lot, but not in summer.

   c It doesn't rain much.

5 According to the brochure, the manor …

   a is new.

   b has changed a lot since it was built.

   c is cold during the night.

6 What does the brochure say that students cannot bring?

   a a waterproof coat

   b an animal

   c lunch

7 Who would the course be suitable for?

   a Someone who just wants to focus on learning English, and doesn't like physical exercise.

   b Someone who loves nature and travel, and wants to learn English.

   c Someone who loves to visit big cities when they travel.

3 What do words 1–5 refer to? Look at the words in bold in the text.

1 These (line 7) ....

2 here (line 20) ....

3 it (line 23) ....

4 These (line 25) ....

5 It (line 30) ....

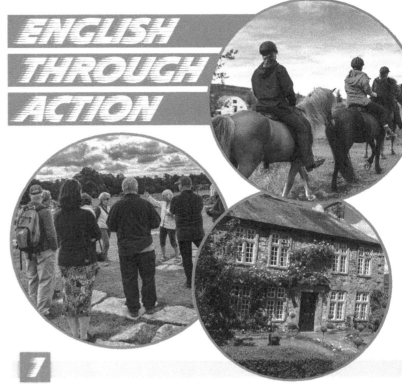

ENGLISH THROUGH ACTION

1 Do you want to improve your English quickly? Do you enjoy doing activities in the fresh air of the countryside? Would you like to spend some time away from home? If the answer is yes to any of these questions, then *English through action* have the course for you!

5 *English through action* offers many different classes to suit your language needs, including general English, business English and exam specific classes with experienced teachers. **These** are held all week, from 9 a.m. to 1 p.m., with a short break for lunch so that you have time to join in the activities in the afternoon and evening. Classes usually
10 have between 15 and 25 students. You don't have to do homework, but here at *English through action* we would suggest that you do as much study as you can during the course.

3

England is well-known for its beautiful scenery and close to the school we have sandy beaches, thick forests and steep hills – perfect for hiking,
15 rock climbing, horse-riding, cycling and hill walking. Each afternoon (from Monday to Friday), groups will do a different outdoor activity with experienced guides who know the area well. Activities will be suited to your preferences and fitness level, and are perfect for nature lovers and those who want to get fit! Remember, however, that it does rain a lot
20 **here**, even in the summer, so you will need to bring a waterproof jacket, walking boots and clothes suitable for outdoor activities.

During your course, you will stay in Main Manor which was built in 1907. Thankfully, **it** has not changed much since then! This does mean, however, that it can be a little cold at night. All meals are
25 included in the price except lunch which is extra. **These** are served in the main hall. Unfortunately, pets are not allowed at the manor.

Tours of the local area and landmarks are held every Friday evening. Local attractions include The Big Adventure Park, the Cathedral and Landwork Castle. This was built in the 1500s and is famous for its blue
30 colour. **It** is visited by thousands of people every year.

Writing

1 Read Charlie's email. What are the positive and negative things he mentions about moving to Spain?

2a Read the email again. Write the words in bold in the correct place in the table below.

Adding ideas	Contrasting ideas
As well as	On the one hand

b Read the Focus box and check your answers.

Adding and contrasting ideas

There are many useful words and phrases you can use when you're adding or contrasting ideas in a piece of writing.

Adding ideas

The people are *also* really friendly **and** the weather on the coast is great all year long.

As well as speaking the language, I love the food and culture.

I love the food and culture. **Besides**, I'm a big fan of surfing.

I'll be far from my family and friends here in England and I know I'll miss them. I *also* haven't found a job yet.

Please write soon and give me advice. Oh, and tell me how your life is, **too**!

Plus, companies want somebody who speaks fluent Spanish and I don't.

Contrasting ideas

It will be a big change, **but** I've been thinking about it for so long.

I also haven't found a job yet, **even though** I've been looking.

On the one hand, the people are warm and welcoming.

On the other hand, I'll be far from my family and friends.

Hi Leo,

I thought I would write and tell you about my news.
Well, you know how much I love Spain. I'm thinking of moving there! It will be a big change, **but** I've been thinking about it for so long and I think I'm almost ready to make the move.

There are so many reasons why I want to go. **As well as** speaking the language, I love the food and culture. The people are **also** really friendly **and** the weather on the coast is great all year long. **Besides**, I'm a big fan of surfing, and there are lots of big waves in places like Tarifa.

There are some disadvantages though that I need to think more about. **On the one hand**, the people are warm and welcoming. **On the other hand**, I'll be far from my family and friends here in England and I know I'll miss them. I also haven't found a job yet, **even though** I've been looking, and moving country is expensive. **Plus**, companies want somebody who speaks fluent Spanish and I don't. In spite of the fact that I've been studying really hard, I'm still not fluent enough. Well, not yet anyway. I suppose that's the biggest problem.

I just can't decide. What do you think? Please write soon and give me advice. Oh, and tell me your news, **too**!

Charlie

3 Combine the sentences with the words in brackets.
1 You love the culture. You love the food. (and)
   You love the culture and the food.
2 You'll meet new friends. You'll learn new skills. (as well as)

3 Moving to Spain will be stressful. You'd be bored if you stayed here. (on the one hand/on the other hand)

4 You might feel lonely. There will be lots of opportunities to meet people. (even though)

Prepare

4 You're going to write an email to a friend asking for advice about one of the topics below. Choose one and make a list of the advantages and disadvantages of doing it.
- Moving to a new city or country
- Buying a house or renting a new apartment
- Doing an intensive English language course in the summer

Write

5 Write an email to your friend and ask for advice using your notes in Exercise 4. Include at least three linkers from the Focus box to help you.

Vocabulary

Shopping

1 **Choose the correct alternatives.**

> I love shopping. I'm practically a professional shopper. My friends think I spend too much money on things like clothes and holidays, but they don't understand that I ¹*save up for/pay for* things that I want to buy. Before I spend my money, I ²*get/look for* bargains and special offers. I love a good ³*refund/deal!* I usually ⁴*wait for/cancel* the sales to buy anything, especially the January sales and Black Friday. That's when almost everything ⁵*gets/goes* on sale!

> Internet shopping is really popular these days, but I hate buying ⁶*goods/receipts* online. I always pay for everything ⁷*by credit card/in cash* with money I can see, and I never pay for anything ⁸*in cash/ by credit card* – I don't even have one! I'm very careful. I always ⁹*keep/look for* the receipts in case I want to exchange anything or get ¹⁰*an order/a refund* – in cash of course!

2 **Complete the sentences with a word or phrase from box A and a word or phrase from box B.**

> A   cancel   get   go   keep   look for   ~~pay for~~
> save up for   wait for

> B   bargains   ~~goods~~   holiday   on sale   order
> receipts   refund   sales

1 I prefer to _____*pay for*_____ my _____*goods*_____ in cash instead of by credit card.
2 They love going to markets at the weekend to
_____ .
3 We're trying to _____ a
_____ in August. We'd love to go to the US. It's difficult, but we try to save £300 every month.
4 Items like clothes and electrical appliances
_____ in January.
5 Lisa waited for four months for delivery. In the end, she had to _____ her _____ .
6 You should always _____ your _____ in case you want to bring something back and get a refund.
7 I'm not buying that now. I'm going to _____ the _____ . It will be much cheaper then!
8 If I were you, I'd call and talk to the manager. If the appliance doesn't work, you should _____ a
_____ .

Grammar

The passive: all tenses

3 **Match the sentence halves.**

1 Your order _____
2 All receipts _____
3 The best bargains _____
4 Your money _____
5 £100,000 worth of goods _____
6 Many huge shopping centres _____

a have been built here over the years.
b has been cancelled.
c are found at weekend markets.
d is being refunded right now.
e have been kept safely in this box.
f were stolen in the robbery.

4 **Rewrite the active sentences in the passive form. Use *by* when necessary.**

1 Staff have lost their jobs.
   Jobs have been lost.
2 People bought a lot of goods from local farmers and shops in the past.
   _____
3 A lot of people pay for purchases online.
   _____
4 High street shops must make changes.
   _____
5 In the future, people will not use cash.
   _____
6 Robots may soon deliver packages.
   _____

5 **Rewrite the passive sentences as active sentences.**

1 Due to the wait, orders were cancelled by customers.
   Customers cancelled orders due to the wait.
2 Credit cards are being used instead of cash by a lot of people today.
   _____
3 The drinks have been paid for by the man over there.
   _____
4 Everything will be done by computers in the future.
   _____
5 Mobile apps that choose our clothes and food for us may soon be developed by companies.
   _____
6 Paper receipts were given to customers by staff.
   _____
7 He was being followed by the detective.
   _____
8 The work has to be done by Friday.
   _____

Vocabulary

Strong and weak adjectives

1 Complete the text with the adjectives in the box.

> disgusting excellent exhausted furious huge
> terrfied thrilled tiny

Terrance loved camping. One summer, he decided to go camping in the Rocky Mountain National Park, a **1**_____ area in Colorado. When he reached the camp, he was **2**_____ and it was dark. He put up his tent and went straight to bed. In the middle of the night, Terrance was woken up by a noise. He looked outside, but he couldn't see anything. There was a **3**_____ smell, so he grabbed his torch and went to investigate … and walked straight into something warm and soft. He switched on his torch and when he saw what it was, he was **4**_____ . He had walked into a big, black bear! He wanted to run, but suddenly he remembered something he had read about black bears. If he ran, the **5**_____ bear might follow him! Slowly, he reached into his pocket and found some chocolate. The book had said that black bears liked chocolate. He threw it into the woods and he was **6**_____ when the bear followed. After, he ran to his car and drove away quickly. He was lucky that he had an **7**_____ memory and had remembered about the chocolate! When he went back the next morning, the bear had gone, but so had his tent. The only things left were **8**_____ pieces of the tent .

2 Read the list of strong adjectives and complete the table with weak adjectives which have a similar meaning.

	Strong adjectives	Weak adjectives
1	tiny	s _mall_
2	furious	a_____
3	thrilled	h_____
4	exhausted	t_____
5	huge	b_____
6	disgusting	b_____
7	terrified	s_____
8	excellent	g_____

Grammar

Third conditional

3 Cross out the extra word in each sentence.
1 We wouldn't have known if he hadn't ~~have~~ told us.
2 If they hadn't have been so exhausted, they would have gone to the party.
3 If Jim had to studied harder at school, he would have passed his exams.
4 Would have things have changed if she had won?
5 The teacher wouldn't have been so furious if you would had done your homework properly.
6 If he hadn't reminded me, if I might have forgotten to call.
7 If I wouldn't have spoken to him if I had known who he was.
8 What would have had happened if he hadn't met your mother?

4 Complete the sentences using the third conditional.
1 I didn't know you were in hospital. I didn't visit you.
   If I had _known you were in hospital, I would have visited you._
2 They were late. They missed the concert.
   If they hadn't _____
3 I moved to Brazil. I met Charlie.
   If I hadn't _____
4 Tom didn't study. He failed his exams.
   If Tom had _____
5 He ran away. The bear didn't kill him.
   If he hadn't _____

5 Connect the actions using the third conditional.
1 Ben woke up late → he missed his bus
   If Ben hadn't woken up late, he wouldn't have missed his bus.
2 he was late for work → his boss fired him
3 Ben lost his job → he decided to go to the beach
4 he decided to go to the beach → he met his ex-girlfriend there
5 he met his ex-girlfriend again → they fell in love again

53

Vocabulary

Describing art

1a Choose the correct alternatives.

Snowdog Art Trails

Snowdog sculptures are individually painted by famous and unknown artists. That means that each snowdog is different and ¹*original/ugly* even though they share a common theme and are based on the story of The Snowman and the Snowdog. Many of the snowdogs are painted in bright colours, making them very ²*old-fashioned/colourful* and ³*cheerful/realistic*. Other snowdogs are more ⁴*realistic/spectacular* and look like real dogs.

Each snowdog is unique and even if you don't like art, it is ⁵*weird/fascinating* to read about the story behind each sculpture. Each story is different and often has a ⁶*unoriginal/powerful* message.

The sculptures are placed around cities at different points and you can buy a map and follow the route, discovering new snowdogs on the way. It's a really ⁷*creative/awful* way to bring art to the public, and lots of people love it.

b Complete the sentences using the pairs of words in the box.

creative/weird   colourful/cheerful   ugly/awful
~~old fashioned/traditional~~   realistic/original

1 Maybe I'm _old fashioned_, but I prefer ___traditional___ art. I just don't like modern art much.
2 She says it's _____, but I just think it's _____. I don't understand what it is.
3 Her painting of the horse was very _____ – it looked like a real one. It wasn't exactly _____, though – I've seen hundreds of paintings like that.
4 It's such a _____ piece, lots of reds, blues and yellows. I look at it when I'm sad, because it's such a _____ image.
5 We didn't like her new one. My friend said it was _____, and I just thought it was really _____ .

Grammar

Short responses with *so, neither/nor, too/either*

2 Complete the conversations with the phrases in the boxes.

Me neither   Me too   So have I

A: Have you seen his new film? It was terrible. I didn't like it at all.
B: ¹_____ . I actually left the cinema before it had finished. If I'd known it was so bad, I wouldn't have gone to see it! I was quite surprised though, I love that actor.
A: ²_____ . He usually picks really good roles. I've seen every other film he's been in!
B: ³_____ !

I didn't either   I do too   Nor do I

A: How's work? Have you finished the project?
B: No. Things are so busy at the moment. I'm always at work. I don't have time to relax, even at the weekends!
A: ⁴_____ . I always have something to do. I really need a holiday.
B: ⁵_____ . It's been ages since I had one. I didn't even go on holiday last summer!
A: ⁶_____ ! Things need to change.

Neither have I   So are we

A: Would you believe that I've never been to an art exhibition?
B: ⁷_____ ! Why don't we go to the exhibition in the Modern Art Museum next week?
A: Next week? I can't. My husband and I have to go to a birthday party. We're so busy at the moment.
B: ⁸_____ . Another time then.

3 Complete the responses.

1 I'm not interested in modern art.
   Neither _____ I.
2 I think this place is really boring.
   So _____ I.
3 I didn't go to work on Tuesday.
   Me _____ .
4 I think his paintings are awful and unoriginal.
   I _____ . I think they're great.
5 I've never been to Buenos Aires.
   I _____ . I went last year.
6 I'm really creative. I love painting and drawing.
   Me _____ . I love spending the afternoon drawing.
7 I didn't like his last novel.
   Neither _____ I.
8 I've wanted to see his art exhibition for ages.
   So _____ I.

Functional language

Make complaints

1 Match the sentence halves.

1 I'm sorry but   *1*
2 The thing is my   ___
3 There seems to be a problem   ___
4 I'd like to speak   ___
5 We'll give you   ___
6 Please could you   ___

a there's a problem with my room.
b to the manager.
c order hasn't arrived.
d with my package.
e bring the bill?
f a refund.

2 Complete the conversations with the phrases from the box.

> bring me the bill   I'm afraid   seems to be   Unfortunately I
> about that   Can I   help you

1 A: Can I ¹_____?
   B: Yes, ²_____ there's something wrong with the torch I bought here yesterday.
   A: What ³_____ the problem?
   B: It doesn't work.
   A: I'm very sorry ⁴_____ . We'll give you a refund.

2 A: Hi. I don't like to complain, but I've been waiting 30 minutes for my dessert! Could you bring it now?
   B: Hm. ⁵_____ can't, we don't have any desserts left.
   A: What? But I've been waiting for 30 minutes! ⁶_____ see the manager, please? I'd like to make a complaint.
   B: Yes, of course.
   A: Oh, and could you ⁷_____ although I'm not paying for the dessert!

3 Put the conversation in the correct order.

a Hi, Customer services, can I help you?   *1*
b Sure. My name is Bobby Ridge, and my account number is 524436.   ___
c That's great, sir. So what seems to be the problem?   ___
d Yes, I seem to have a problem with my phone bill.   ___
e The thing is, there's an extra $20 on my bill this month, and I don't know why.   ___
f OK, sir, can I have your name and account details?   ___
g OK, sir. Please could you hold the line while I check your account charges?   ___
h Hello, Mr Ridge. It seems to be a mistake with your bill. We'll refund you the $20 immediately.   ___
i Sure, no problem.   ___
j Ah, I see. Well, that's fine. Thank you very much for your help.   ___

Listening

1 🔊 9.01 **Listen to four conversations and match them with situations a–d.**
a A tour guide explaining something   *4*
b An unhappy shopper   ___
c Friends deciding on an exhibition   ___
d A couple deciding on something in their home   ___

2 Listen again and choose the correct alternatives to complete the sentences.

Conversation 1
The couple agree to hang the painting in …
a the bathroom.
b the bedroom.
c the hall.

Conversation 2
The man in the shop wants …
a his money back.
b to exchange the frame.
c to speak to the person who sold him the painting.

Conversation 3
The friends decide to go to …
a the sculpture exhibition.
b neither exhibition.
c the photography exhibition.

Conversation 4
The tour guide is describing the …
a material used in the sculpture.
b relationship between the people in the sculpture.
c death of the artist.

3 Listen again and match conversations 1–4 with statements a–d.

1 Someone wants a piece of art to be easy to see.   ___
2 One person doesn't like a certain type of art.   ___
3 One person is discussing what a piece of art means.   ___
4 A piece of art is damaged.   ___

Reading

1 Read the text and complete it with the names of famous sculptures in the box.

> Newton   OY or YO?   First Generation sculpture
> The Sagrada Familia chocolate sculpture
> The Shoes on the Danube Bank

2 Read the text again and answer the questions.
Which sculpture:

1 reflects how poor or rich a group of people are?

....

2 tells a different story of a public figure?

....

3 remembers a group of people from a difficult time
  in history?

....

4 doesn't use typical material for the sculpture?

....

5 reflects the multicultural world we live in?

....

3 Read the text again and choose the correct meaning of the words.

1 interpreted (paragraph 1)
  a understood
  b changed into a foreign language

2 passerby (paragraph 1)
  a person who has decided to visit a particular place
  b person who is going past a particular place

3 didn't have very much (paragraph 2)
  a didn't have much time
  b didn't have much money

4 frozen in time (paragraph 2)
  a staying the same way forever
  b really cold for a very long time

5 is the place for you (paragraph 3)
  a is the best place for you to go
  b the only place you can visit

6 look closely (paragraph 4)
  a look quickly
  b look carefully

7 based on (paragraph 4)
  a using ideas from
  b living in that area

8 reflect on (paragraph 5)
  a think about
  b see yourself

9 touching (paragraph 5)
  a making you feel sad or emotional
  b putting your hand on something

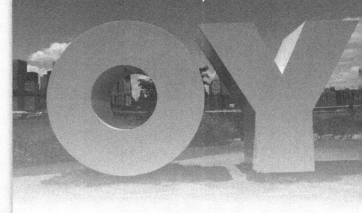

Love or hate modern art, you will certainly have an opinion about these weird and wonderful sculptures. We've chosen just a few from around the world for you to choose from.

1 .... has an interesting concept; depending on where you are standing you'll read two different words. It's clear that language plays a big part in this sculpture. The two words are also important because they are now part of so many languages around the world. The words can be **interpreted** in various ways, including a modern way of saying hello, and a way of getting someone's attention. It's also possible that this structure represents the ethnic and cultural diversity in the different neighbourhoods in New York. But of course, like any form of public art, it's for the **passerby** to decide.

2 .... was created in 2000 and is considered one of the most original sculptures in Singapore. It shows a group of five boys jumping into the river. They're thought to be the first immigrants in the country who used the river as a huge swimming pool. According to the sculptor, the river was a playground for those who **didn't have very much**, but found enjoyment and adventure there. It shows positive feelings of a moment of happiness **frozen in time**. It's an image of humanity and hope.

3 .... is an unusual (and sweet) piece of artwork located in a small, private museum in Barcelona. If you like art, history … and sweet foods, then this **is the place for you**. You could eat most of the sculptures here, but I'm not sure you would be popular with the museum if you did! You'll also learn about well-known buildings in the city. Just don't eat them!

The **4** .... sculpture can be found in the British Library's courtyard. The figure is the father of the Enlightenment. But this tribute to the great man is not very traditional if you **look closely**. The sculpture was **based on** a picture by a famous artist, William Blake, who didn't like all of Newton's ideas.

5 .... is the least cheerful sculpture on our list, but it's an important memorial to honour the victims of the fascist regime in World War II. The shoes represent the lives lost at the banks of the river in Budapest, Hungary. There are 60 pairs of shoes made of iron. Any passerby will stop and **reflect on** this sad period in history. A powerful exhibition and a **touching** memorial.

9

Writing

1 **Read the story and put the events in the correct order.**

  a moved to Spain ....

  b finished university   _1_

  c went on holiday to Andalucía ....

  d met her friend ....

  e started teaching ....

  f moved to Málaga ....

  g met someone at a conference ....

I sometimes think my life started with a phone call. It was 2002 and I'd finished university and applied for a job as a teaching assistant in France. I went for an interview, but didn't get the job. One sunny morning in July, I got a phone call – the person they'd offered the job to couldn't go to France, so they asked if I'd like to go instead. I couldn't believe it – I was like an excited schoolchild!

I always think about that person who didn't take the job. If he'd accepted it, I would never have gone to France, and if I hadn't gone to France, I wouldn't have become a teacher. I loved it and my first group of children were fantastic!

I stayed in France for two years and then moved to the capital of Spain. I still remember my first day there, it was summer, and the city was as hot as an oven. On that first day I met a very good friend, Frankie, and, on one summer holiday, she took me to Andalucía in the south of Spain. Málaga soon became my holiday escape when I needed to get away from the city. Frankie had a beautiful villa in the hills and I used to love going there to relax.

After years of living in the city, I decided that I was tired from a stressful job and city life. I saw an advert for a teaching position in Málaga and I decided that the time was right to move. It was the best decision I've ever made. I'm writing this on my balcony on another sunny day. I can see the sea from here. It's so beautiful – it looks like a mirror. I thank Frankie. If I hadn't met her, I would never have come.

2 **Read the Focus box and rewrite the sentences using the words in brackets.**

Making comparisons

We can use comparisons to make a piece of writing more interesting. There are different ways to do this.

We can use *as ... as* to say that one thing is similar to something else, often using an adjective.

*The city was **as hot as** an oven.*

We can also use *like* to say that two things are similar.

*I was **like** an excited schoolchild!*

If we want to focus on appearance, we can use *look like*.

We can use it with a noun or a clause.

*It's so beautiful – it **looks like** a mirror.*

*He **looked like** he was having fun.*

  1 My grandad's hair is really white, like snow. (as)

  ....

  2 From the plane, the people reminded me of ants. (look)

  ....

  3 He's so cold sometimes. He's like ice. (as)

  ....

  4 She was similar to a summer's day, because she was so sweet. (as)

  ....

Prepare

3a **You're going to write about an event which changed your life. Choose an event from the box or one of your own.**

moving to a new place   taking a job
deciding not to do something   meeting someone

  b **Write some sentences using comparisons to help describe the situation.**

  I was as white as a sheet on my first day at work, because I was so nervous.

Write

4 **Write your story. Include your sentences from Exercise 3 and use the Focus box to help you.**

57

Vocabulary
Education

1 **Choose the correct option a, b or c.**

1 I'm so nervous about tomorrow that I can't sleep. I hate _____ exams!

   a taking   b attending   c revising

2 My sister went to a boarding school, but I _____ a state school.

   a go   b attend   c pay

3 If you don't pay attention in class, you won't _____ high grades.

   a pass   b fail   c get

4 It can be quite difficult to _____ good enough qualifications to study medicine.

   a fail   b study   c get

5 Sorry, I can't meet you this weekend. I have to _____ for my summer exams.

   a revise   b take   c pay

6 I think it is terrible that we have to _____ such high fees for university or college.

   a give   b pay   c do

7 If we do well and _____ our exams, we'll have to go out and celebrate!

   a fail   b sit   c pass

8 In some private schools, students don't have to _____ exams or tests.

   a take   b revise   c have

2 **Match the sentence halves.**

1 I'd love to go to boarding   _c_

2 A lot of families are happy to pay high school   _____

3 I didn't get good grades at school, but   _____

4 I have good qualifications in   _____

5 I didn't always attend all my   _____

6 If I fail the   _____

7 Some of my friends went to private   _____

8 Patrick didn't revise much   _____

a maths, biology and physics.

b test, I'll just take it again.

c school. It would be so much fun to live and study in the same place.

d I've been very successful in my career.

e fees because they want their children to get the best education.

f for his German exam, but he still got a very high grade for it!

g university classes. Sometimes I stayed in bed.

h school, and some went to state school.

Grammar
Reported statements

3 **Rewrite the direct speech as reported statements.**

1 'I passed my exams!', said Lisa.
   Lisa said _she had passed her exams_ .

2 'The best idea is to study hard for tests', said the teacher.
   The teacher said _____ .

3 'We attended private school', they said.
   They told me _____ .

4 'I'm revising for my exams, so I can't go', said James.
   James told us _____ .

5 'Universities will be free for everybody in the future', said the mayor.
   The mayor said that _____ .

6 'The new teacher has really helped us', said Dan and Mark.
   Dan and Mark told me _____ .

7 'We don't want to pay more college fees', the students say.
   The students say _____ .

8 'We need more money and more time to plan our lessons', said the group of teachers.
   The group of teachers said _____ .

4 **Correct the mistake in each reported statement.**

1 'I'm not happy!'

   He told ~~to~~ me he wasn't happy.

2 'We will leave and get new jobs.'

   They told us we would leave and get new jobs.

3 'I'm revising for a test.'

   She told me she revises for a test.

4 'I don't like boarding schools.'

   He said he hadn't liked boarding schools.

5 'We have graduated from university.'

   They said they graduated from university.

6 'We enjoyed primary school.'

   They told her they have enjoyed primary school.

7 'Studying together will help us pass our exams.'

   They told me studying together does help them pass their exams.

Vocabulary

Suggestions and improvements

1 **Choose the correct alternatives.**

1 'Let's go on a city break for your birthday,' he *advised/ suggested*.
2 'Don't go down there, it's dangerous!' she *promised/ warned*.
3 'I'll do it tomorrow,' he *encouraged/promised*.
4 'If I were you, I'd go to the doctor,' she *advised/convinced*.
5 'We need to reduce bus fares for people over 60! Now!' they *demanded/promised*.
6 'You should try the new Italian restaurant in town,' he *recommended/refused*.

2 **Complete the sentences with the words in the box.**

> avoided   considered   persuaded   promised
> recommended   refused   started   warned

1 The government has _____ answering some very serious questions.
2 The mayor has _____ everyone to cycle more. Good for him!
3 He _____ to eat green vegetables and do regular exercise. That's why he got sick.
4 They _____ offering people free meals, but then they changed their minds.
5 People have _____ to cycle on the pavement. We need to stop them!
6 Police _____ people not to drive today because of the heavy snow.
7 He _____ not to go too fast in his car again, after his accident.
8 I _____ going there by train, as it's faster.

Grammar

Verb patterns

3 **Choose the correct option a, b or c.**

1 We recommend _____ public transport and leaving your car at home at least twice a month.
   a using   b to use   c use
2 The town should promise _____ more cycle lanes.
   a providing   b provide   c to provide
3 Nowadays, everybody is encouraged _____ glass, paper and plastic.
   a recycle   b to recycle   c recycling
4 Their best friend Jasper persuaded _____ to the country.
   a them moving   b them to move   c them move
5 I really recommend _____ there next summer.
   a going   b you to go   c go
6 We suggest _____ all electrical appliances before going to bed.
   a you switching off   b you to switch off
   c switching off
7 Doctors warn people _____ because it's so bad for your health.
   a don't smoke   b not smoking   c not to smoke
8 The politicians want to avoid _____ anything about the problem.
   a do   b doing   c to do

4 **Rewrite the sentences using the correct form of the verbs in brackets so that they have a similar meaning.**

1 I'll always arrive on time in future. (promise)
   I _____ .
2 I think going on the bus is a good idea. (recommend)
   I _____ .
3 You'll never change my mind about going ice skating. (persuade)
   You'll _____ .
4 Don't eat oily foods – they'll make you feel bad. (avoid)
   You should _____ .
5 Sorry, but I'm not going to another one of his stupid meetings. (refuse)
   Sorry, but I _____ .
6 I think you should travel more. (advise)
   I _____ .
7 I told her she should definitely say something at the meeting. (encourage)
   I _____ .
8 It's a good idea to wait half an hour before leaving. (suggest)
   She _____ .
9 No one arrives at the office before nine. (start)
   People _____ .
10 Don't go there at night. (warn)
   He _____ .

Vocabulary

Work activities

1 Complete the sentences with the words in the box.

> interview people   write reports
> do research   set up meetings
> give presentations   serve customers
> work in a team

1 My job is really tiring. I clean tables, take orders and _____ all day.

2 I organise everything in the office. When we need new employees, I also _____ if the director doesn't have time to speak to them.

3 People think my job is just about teaching, but you also need to _____ about students and send them to the parents.

4 In my job you need to be confident, organised, responsible and have good communication skills. I often have to _____ to groups of people about projects I'm working on.

5 My job is all about studying the environment and doing experiments. I often have to _____ on particular subjects and write reports about what I've discovered.

6 I'm the first person you see when you enter the office. I know everything that happens here. I do a lot of different things, but I mainly have to answer the phone, take notes and _____ for the boss and other employees.

7 I love my job. Maybe that's because I've always loved cooking! Everybody works together here in the kitchen and you really have to be able to _____ .

2 Match the sentence halves.

1 Could you arrange _____
2 I don't think they'll _____
3 Managing this _____
4 Our company employs _____

a 10,000 people.
b a meeting for me for tomorrow?
c offer me the job.
d project is really tough.

Grammar

Reported questions

3 Put the words and phrases in the correct order to make sentences.

1 Jane / had passed the test / how she / John asked
   John asked Jane how she had passed the test.

2 him / I asked / he recommended studying at the weekend / if
   _____

3 give us an example / We asked / him / to
   _____

4 what / She wanted / to know / I had done in my last job
   _____

5 what / They asked / experience I had / me
   _____

6 me / what / countries I had been to / She asked
   _____

7 why / They asked / I wanted the job / me
   _____

8 He asked / where / I would be in five years' time / me
   _____

4 Rewrite the questions using reported speech.

1 Do you have experience in this area?
   They asked Mike *if he had experience in this area* .

2 Do you enjoy writing reports?
   They asked Mike _____ .

3 Do you have any qualifications?
   They asked Mike _____ .

4 What is your greatest skill?
   They wanted to know _____ .

5 Where were you working last year?
   They asked Mike _____ .

6 Where will you be in ten years' time?
   They asked Mike _____ .

7 Do you like working in a team?
   They wanted to know _____ .

8 Why do you want to work here?
   They asked Mike _____ .

Functional language

Ask and answer interview questions

1 Read the sentences. In an interview who would usually say these things, the interviewer (I) or the candidate (C)?

1 I'd be interested to know how much experience you have in this area. ___*I*___
2 I'm hoping to manage my own projects in the future. _____
3 I think I'd say I'm organised and responsible. _____
4 Can you tell me about your qualifications? _____
5 Where do you see yourself in two years? _____
6 I'd like to get my Masters this year. _____
7 What would you say is your greatest skill? _____
8 What made you decide to leave your last job? _____

2 Put the words in the correct order to complete the conversations.

1 A: What / you / a / decide / made / teacher? / to / become
  1 *What made you decide to become a teacher?*

  B: Well, I've always loved children and teaching is one of the most important jobs you can do!

  A: tell / me / more / your / experience? / Can / you / about
  2 _____

  B: I worked as a teaching assistant for two years and as a full-time teacher for the last six years. I love it!

2 A: So could you describe yourself in just three words?

  B: I / think / responsible / I'd / say / dedicated / and / reliable
  3 _____

  A: That's interesting. Can you tell me something about your skills?

  B: IT / skills / see / from / my / CV / As / you / can / I've / excellent / got
  4 _____

3 A: Why / company? / you / want / to / work / do / for / this
  5 _____

  B: Well, I've always loved technology and this company has a great reputation.

  A: future? / goals / are / your / for / the / What
  6 _____

  B: I hope to manage my own department someday.

  A: So / me? / for / questions / do / you / any / have
  7 _____

  B: Yes, when will I know if I've got the job?

4 A: So final question. me / tell / about / you / Could / your / hobbies?
  8 _____

  B: Sure. I love reading and I am a member of a local cinema club. I also write a regular blog about films.
  3 _____

  A: Sounds great. be / I'd / to / interested / read / it!
  9 _____

Listening

1 🔊 10.01 Listen to a news report on a new *park and ride* service. Number the opinions in the order that you hear them.

a Safety is important. _____

b The location of the *park and ride* is perfect. _____

c *Park and ride* is cheaper than parking. _____

d *Park and ride* is better for the environment. _____

e People drive too quickly. _____

2 Listen again and complete the sentences. Use between one and three words.

1 The council will convert a hotel car park into a _____ .
2 Buses will go every _____ from the car park.
3 The mayor wants to encourage people _____ in the town centre.
4 The first woman says she spends half an hour looking for a _____ .
5 The first man says parking is _____ at the moment.
6 The woman who has driven for 40 years doesn't feel _____ driving anymore.
7 The second man thinks the new *park and ride* will reduce _____ .
8 The reporter says park and share meeting points will be at a pub, _____ or _____ .

Reading

1 **Read the article and choose the best title.**

a A different perspective on education

b An education for everyone

c Education: past and present

What does traditional education mean to you?

Probably very teacher-centred lessons with little communication between the students. You might remember strict teachers and strict rules. You might also think of sitting exams and trying to get the highest marks. We explored two other types of schools to see if there was an alternative to the system we have. Each school has a unique method of teaching, which is far from traditional. Here they are!

Brooklyn Free School is for primary and secondary school students. In fact, its youngest students are only four. The school's philosophy is very different from traditional education. To give you an idea: imagine a school where the students make the rules and choose their classes. More surprisingly, they have a policy which means students don't have to go to class if they don't want to. They don't have to revise for tests because there aren't any! They don't have to hand in homework every day because they decide if they want to do it or not! This means that at the end of the year, there are no grades. If the child has a problem, he or she can ask for a meeting and discuss it with the entire school. If a student is bored of a subject, such as chemistry, he or she can get up and walk out, or go to the lounge and read a book all day. Some students spend years on 'independent study', where they can do any projects they like. The students are completely independent during this time. Others take classes like screenwriting, architecture or something related to sports. The key concept here seems to be freedom to choose.

Microsoft's School of the Future also breaks from tradition. Even the building looks like something out of the future! You might guess from the name of this school that every student needs a laptop to attend this public secondary school in Philadelphia. The system in this school prepares students for the digital world of work when they finish school. Instead of textbooks, students use their laptops, and new technologies are used in the classrooms. This school also encourages children to participate in arts and music. There's a school choir and band and students can continue with these activities if they show real talent. For students who attend classes and show good behaviour, there are rewards and events to show them that doing well in school can be fun. The fees aren't cheap, but you don't have to buy textbooks and by sending your children here, you're also helping the environment.

Like everything else in the world today, education is changing and perhaps these schools are leading the way!

2 **Read the article again. Are the sentences true (T) or false (F)?**

1 At the Brooklyn Free School, students can help decide how the school works. ....

2 At the Brooklyn Free School, students are not allowed to do homework. ....

3 At the Brooklyn Free School, students can choose their classes. ....

4 At the Brooklyn Free School, the students get a grade based on a project they complete. ....

5 At Microsoft's School of the Future, students don't use textbooks. ....

6 At Microsoft's School of the Future, there are rewards for good behaviour. ....

7 It's expensive to attend Microsoft's School of the Future. ....

8 Students have less freedom in these schools than in regular schools. ....

3 **Read the sentences. Do they refer to *Brooklyn Free School* (B) or *Microsoft School of the Future* (M)**

1 'I like the fact that sending Johnny to this school helps to reduce the amount of paper that is used.' _M_

2 'I'm too young to attend it now, but I hope to go there when I'm eleven.' ....

3 'I like it because I have more choice about what I do than in a regular school.' ....

4 'If we work hard and get good results they give us nice things or take us to interesting places.' ....

5 'I sometimes worry that my child might decide not to do any study at all.' ....

6 'Sheetal loves singing, so she's really going to enjoy singing with the other students.' ....

7 'When I first saw the school, I thought it looked like something from a science fiction film.' ....

8 'Next year I'm going to build a car. That's all I'm going to do.' ....

9 'There are lots of non-traditional subjects. That's great, because I hate English and maths.' ....

10 'If I have a problem, I can discuss it with everyone else and we can find a solution.' ....

Writing

1 Read the email and answer the questions.

1 What would Daisuke like to learn?

_____

_____

2 Why doesn't he want to use his own violin?

_____

_____

3 Why can he only study late at night?

_____

_____

4 Why does he want to pay for more than one class at the same time?

_____

_____

_____

○ ● ●

[1]Dear Ms Adams,

[2]I am writing to ask for more information about the private violin lessons which you offer. I have recently seen your advert in the St Leonards Chronicle.

Firstly, **[3]I would like to know if** I need to bring my own violin. The one I have at home is quite old and not very good, and I would prefer to use one of yours, if possible.

Secondly, I have a question about your timetable. Please could you send me some details about when I can do these lessons? I work until 9 p.m. most days, so I'd prefer something after 10 p.m. I hope that's not too late.

[4]Could you also let me know if I can get a discount if I pay for more than one lesson at the same time? I saw that your lessons cost 30 euros an hour, but if I book five lessons would it be possible to pay 25 euros an hour?

[5]I look forward to hearing from you and thank you in advance for your time.

[6]Yours sincerely,

Daisuke Matsumoto

2 Read the email again and match informal phrases a–f with phrases with a similar meaning in bold in the email. Use the Focus box to help you.

a Hi ___1___

b Bye _____

c Also, tell me if _____

d Write soon _____

e I'm writing for info about _____

f I want to know if _____

Requesting information

When we write an email requesting information, we often structure it in the following way.

Say why you are writing.

I am writing to ask for information about …

I am writing to find out more about …

I am writing to enquire about …

Ask detailed questions and make requests.

I would also like to know if …

Could you also let me know if/ what/ when …?

Could you advise me …?

Please could you send me details about …

I would be grateful if you would/ could …

End your email.

I look forward to hearing from you.

Thank you in advance.

Prepare

3a You have recently seen an advert online for Scottish dance classes. Write some questions you might want to ask the teacher. Use the ideas below to help you.

1 Timetable

How often are the lessons?

2 Price

_____

_____

3 Experience

_____

_____

4 Clothing

_____

_____

b Read the Focus box and underline some expressions that you'd like to use in your email.

Write

4 Write the email using your notes in Exercise 3 and the Focus box to help you.

AUDIO SCRIPTS

P = Presenter   M = Michael

P: Here in the studio we have Michael, a researcher from Kent University, talking to us about the future of homeworking. Good morning, Michael, and thank you for joining us today.

M: Thank you for inviting me.

P: So there has been a lot of debate about the advantages and disadvantages of homeworking. Is it a good thing, Michael?

M: Well, there are a few things to consider, for example the social impact and also the big question of the environment.

P: OK, so let's start with the social factor. Do you think homeworking will affect relationships?

M: Certainly. Working in an office means we have contact with other people and make friendships which we then enjoy outside the office. If we start working from home, we will lose this contact.

P: Of course, but it is getting easier to meet people online as social networking sites are always improving … and increasing in number!

M: That's true, but I'm also thinking more about the benefits of working with other people in the same space. We sometimes get our ideas from talking to our colleagues, and if we're working alone, I don't see how we can collaborate and share ideas so easily.

P: But there are so many ways we can talk to each other without being face to face, aren't there? The phone, for example?

M: Yes, but ideas and solutions often come up outside of meetings. You might be having a coffee with a colleague and just by talking, an idea comes to you.

P: Well, that's certainly true. OK, so let's talk about the environment. How is that connected to homeworking?

M: There has been some interesting research here. We often think working from home saves on carbon, I mean, if you think about how many cars are on the road as people travel to work …

P: Well, we definitely need to reduce the number of cars …

M: We do; we all know how much time we waste in traffic jams, too, but we also have to consider other forms of energy. Take the example of heating. To heat an office for a group of employees in the winter is more efficient than heating a house for one person.

P: Yes, I don't fancy working in a cold house in the winter.

M: Exactly. Obviously, we have to remember that in the summer, a homeworker wouldn't be putting on their heating.

P: Does that mean we could do both? Work in an office in the winter and work from home in the warmer months?

M: That could be one solution, yes.

P: And how about business owners? I imagine they're not keen on their employees working from home?

M: This is another issue; many bosses don't like managing people they can't see as they worry about losing control. I think proper training for managers could make a difference here. We have to consider the happiness of employees, too.

P: It's true to say there is a definite connection between being happy at work and being productive.

M: Without a doubt. We all know that if we are happy, we feel more motivated to work. Motivation is the key to being more productive. Managers have to recognise this if they want a more productive company, and one way to make employees happier is by giving them less stressful and more comfortable working conditions.

P: Well, that sounds good to me. I might speak to my boss later about working from home myself!

D = David   H = Holly   C= Claudia

David

My most vivid memory? That's an easy one! When we were kids, my brothers and I used to play in the fields behind our house after school. We had so much fun. We used to spend hours there, running around and playing together. One afternoon, while we were playing football, we suddenly looked up to see a herd of cows … running straight towards us! We all looked at each other in shock and then ran away as fast as we could. By the time we reached our house, we were exhausted … but we were safe! I'll never forget how frightened we felt, and of course we never played in those fields again! It's strange but the smell of freshly cut grass always takes me back to that moment.

Holly

I moved to Shenzhen in China to teach English for a year in 1988. In the beginning, it was tough and a bit stressful as I had to work long hours and I didn't have any friends at that point. I thought I would feel homesick for the whole time I was there, but, actually, in the end I had a fantastic experience. I really liked my job and my students were great. Soon, I started to discover a new culture and meet lots of new and interesting people. I even began to learn the language … And the food! The food was the best part. It was incredible. I had so much fun trying local dishes. My favourite was congee, a creamy rice soup. It smells so good. In fact every time I have it now, it brings back memories of that time!

Claudia

My most memorable experience? Well, it would have to be the time I met my hero, the writer Rick Stevens. I had been a fan of his books for years and I used to wait excitedly for every new book to be released. One day, I was walking down the street when suddenly, there he was, in my local bookshop. Imagine that! I was so surprised … and I don't know how, but I walked up to him and asked if I could send him some of my writing … and he agreed! He actually helped to start my career! Now I write for a local newspaper and I'm currently writing my first novel! It's funny, but I'll always remember the song by Kylie Minogue that was playing in the bookshop that day. Every time I hear it on the radio now, it reminds me of how lucky I was!

One

I've met so many amazing people, I suppose because I've done a lot of travelling and I've never stayed in one place for too long. In fact, I've lived in 20 cities so far! I travel because of my job, and it's easy to make friends with colleagues because you see them a lot, every day in the office. It's harder with my childhood friends. We don't see each other much and staying in touch is not as easy as you would think, even with all the new technologies and social media we have. We also have very different lives: most of my friends have never left my hometown and some have had families early. However, we do make sure that at the beginning of each New Year we look in our diaries to find one weekend when we can all get together that year. Normally, we do a city break so it's like a reunion and a mini holiday! It's fabulous to meet up in a different place and there's always so much to catch up on!

Two

I love meeting new people, and I have different groups of friends from each stage of my life. I have my school friends, then friendships from university and one or two friends from each job I've had – there have been a few! When I was younger, I kept in touch with people by phone. I used to spend every Sunday calling old friends, wherever I was; it was my Sunday routine! I loved writing letters, too, but I don't do it now, I guess very few people do. I do write occasional emails to friends, though, telling them my news. To be honest, these days, keeping in touch doesn't take that much effort. 'Liking' a photo or an update on social media is an easy way to show that we care about what is going on in each other's lives. I think saying that life is too busy to keep in touch is an excuse. It's like anything – you make it possible if you really want to.

Three

My dad was in the Air Force so we moved every three years! I quickly got used to meeting new people and now I find it quite easy to make friends. I have made some very good friends, but I only have a couple of friends who I've kept in touch with. I guess because these were special friendships and so I think we'll be friends for life. But I think this is rare. Things change so much in life and it's not realistic to think you'll have things in common with a friend that you had when you were ten. I don't think friendships have to last a lifetime. People come into your life at different moments and when people move on, you should give thanks for the time you had with them.

P = Presenter   L = Luke   A = Amy   Pa = Paul   J = Jo   C = Clem

P: Today in the studio, we are talking about things we couldn't live without and we have five millennials to help us! Let's start with you, Luke. What would be the one thing you can't live without?

L: Apart from my girlfriend? I would have to say my phone. I absolutely love music and can't live without it. I listen to music on my phone on the way to the office, and when I'm at work. I think without music, I would go crazy. Life today can be so stressful and noisy, especially living in a big city, so sometimes I try and stop all the noise with some relaxing music.

P: Thanks, Luke, although I do wonder how a 20-year-old can be stressed. And Amy, you're a researcher in a social media company, so we can guess what your object would be!

A: Actually, you'd be surprised. I would definitely leave social media behind if I went to a desert island. In fact, my research proves that we would be better off without it! Whenever I need to get away, I head for the countryside. I love getting out of the city and need to be active – I think it's so important to do plenty of exercise, especially in the fast-paced world we live in. My big passion is walking, so it would have to be my boots!

P: Paul, over to you. You've recently started your own company I believe?

Pa: That's right, so without my laptop I'd be lost. I use it for everything: for my schedules, for email, talking to people online … I couldn't be without it. It's essential for organising my life. I'm very sociable so I spend hours and hours on social media. It drives my family crazy!

P: Thanks, Paul. Over to you, Jo. What would be your thing?

J: I know it's not really a 'thing', but I think it would have to be online shopping! Especially Netline Direct – definitely my number one shop! I use it all the time as it's so reliable and I don't have to leave the house. I've never been disappointed and the only time I had an issue, the customer service was excellent and the problem was solved in minutes. I always use it for myself or even for buying presents. It means I don't have to go shopping, which is wonderful because shopping is always the last thing I want to do!

P: Thanks, Jo, and last but not least, Clem … what would be the thing you couldn't live without?

C: I'm going to say something very non-tech … a book would be my most precious possession. I read for at least two hours a day, and when I go anywhere I take a book with me. It's the only way I can take a break from this world, and lose myself in a different one. The last book I read was called *The Star Man*. It was amazing and changed my life!

P: Wow! That's saying something. Thanks for all your contributions. It was very interesting to hear what's important to our millennials.

M = Maria   A = Andrew   R = Raquel   B = Brian
G = Gina   T = Tina

Conversation 1

M: Hey, you seem happy – it must be good news!

A: It is actually. The boss has just told me that we're going to have uniforms instead of casual clothes. Starting next month. What a great idea!

M: What? That can't be true. It's a terrible idea.

A: It's a great idea! Think about it, Maria. Uniforms mean that we don't have to spend so much time every morning choosing something to wear to work.

M: Yes, but then we'll all look the same! My clothes are part of my personality, without that we're all just like … robots.

A: I'm sorry you don't like it, Maria, but if you think about it …

M: I don't need to think about it. I'm going to find the boss and tell him what I think. Uniforms!

Conversation 2

R: Hey Brian, I haven't seen you for a while. I thought you were ill or something.

B: Oh no, I just had to take a few days off. I've sold my flat and bought a cottage in the country, so I spent the last few days packing everything up. There was so much more than I thought …

R: I know, we moved last year and I found the whole thing really stressful …

B: Yeah, I had to pack all of my clothes, the furniture, everything, all by myself.
It was crazy.

R: Poor you!

B: Oh, and then when I finally got to the new place, the central heating didn't work!

R: Oh, what did you do?

B: It was OK in the end, but yes, a total nightmare. I'm so tired.

R: Er, yes, it can't be easy for you … oh, that's my phone … I'd better take this, speak to you later!

Conversation 3

G: Oh, it's one o'clock already. Hey Tina, do you want to come for lunch?

T: I'd love to, Gill, but I really can't. I have to go shopping for a new dress for a party at the weekend … and besides, I'm watching what I eat at the moment.

G: Really? But why don't you come and order something like grilled fish and a green salad? The restaurant on the corner has some really healthy options. You can always get the dress after work, come on …

T: Argh, it's just every time I eat out, I have something fried or really unhealthy, like chips or chocolate. I can't stop myself. And then I feel bad after. I hate dieting!

G: You don't need to diet. The key to a balanced diet is eating a little bit of everything – fruit, vegetables, fish … and even sweet things occasionally, having regular meals and doing enough exercise. If you do all that, then you'll be healthy and feel great.

T: Hmm, that's easy to say …

G: Come on, let's go. I'm starving!

T: OK, I'm coming!

UNIT 6 Recording 1

P = Presenter   S = Sharon

P: In the studio today we have Sharon Shane. Sharon is a writer for 'Household' magazine, and today she'll be talking about safety in the home. Sharon … welcome!

S: Thank you for having me!

P: Most accidents actually do happen at home, don't they?

S: Well, yes, exactly, and people can have very serious accidents at home, too. Today I'm going to tell you about the potential dangers in areas of the home like the bathroom, kitchen and the bedroom.

P: Let's start with the bathroom. Now, I actually had an accident the other day. As I got out of the shower, I slipped on the soap. Luckily I put my hand out and stopped myself from falling. If I hadn't, I don't know what would have happened. It was a shock, but luckily I didn't injure myself.

S: Well, exactly and many domestic accidents do occur in the bathroom. Everyone should have a shower mat in the shower or bath tub. This really is very important. You also shouldn't have things on the bathroom floor which you could fall over, especially when you're rushing to get ready for work! When you leave the bathroom, dry the floor so no one can slip on it. These falls can be very unpleasant and occasionally, fatal.

P: Gosh, that sounds dramatic.

S: Well, it can be. There are lots of things in homes that we don't think of as dangerous, but can be. Take the dishwasher, for example, it's often full of sharp objects like knives that children could easily reach. My advice would be to always empty the dishwasher straightaway and never leave the door open. Tidiness and organisation are the most important things when it comes to avoiding danger in the home.

P: OK, this all sounds very logical, but it's easy to see how when we're busy or half asleep, accidents can happen. So, what about the kitchen?

S: Well, a lot of people still have gas in their homes. If you do, then make sure you turn it off as soon as you finish cooking. All other electrical appliances should also be switched off when you're not using them.

P: You can also buy appliances which have built-in security devices, can't you?

S: Yes and I would always pay a little more to have these safer options.

P: OK, so finally, the bedroom. It's easy to think of accidents in the bathroom and kitchen, but the bedroom?

S: Well, you'd be surprised. The other day, I tripped over a pair of shoes that I'd left in the middle of the floor. I was very close to hitting my head on my wardrobe.

P: So, it comes back to tidiness, doesn't it?

S: It really does, yes. If you're like me and you get up a lot in the night to use the bathroom, make sure you tidy up before you turn off your light! If you do get up, switch on your bedside lamp. Getting up in the dark when you're half asleep is an accident waiting to happen.

P: Well, thanks Sharon, I certainly never knew the home could be so dangerous. I'd better get home to do some housework!

UNIT 7 Recording 1

Sarah

I'll never forget my jungle adventure. David, and I have always loved travelling. When we got married, we promised that we'd save in order to take a trip … do something completely new … explore the world. For our first wedding anniversary, David told me he'd organised a surprise and that the surprise was a trip away. I was so excited, but I had no idea where we were going. On the morning we were leaving, he gave me a backpack and some walking boots. He said that I'd need them in order to survive in the jungle! The jungle! Can you believe it? Turns out that he'd booked us a holiday in the Amazon! Three weeks hiking through the jungle. I'd travelled through Europe, but I'd never been to South America. It was, without a doubt, one of the best experiences I've ever had. Definitely the best present ever!

Jude

I've travelled practically everywhere, but I think the most important trip was one I took when I finished university. I had always loved French culture and food, so when I finished, I immediately booked a one-way ticket to Paris to spend the summer there. When I arrived, I took a French course so that I could work on my speaking skills. I studied every morning and practised with the locals in the evenings. I have such great memories of that time ... lazy days walking through the streets, happy hours spent exploring the museums and delightful evenings spent trying all of the delicious food. That summer really taught me a lot about the country, the culture and the people. I haven't been back since ... and I don't think I want to return ... I've heard that it has changed a lot. I want the Paris of that summer to stay exactly the same in my memory ... perfect.

Georgina

My most important trip? Let's see. Well, there was that time in Berlin ... and then there was that time in Sydney ... no ... wait. It has to be the first camping trip that I went on with my parents ... years ago ... for my birthday. We spent five days by the sea, in the north of England. I don't remember everything ... I was only seven ... but I do remember very happy times spent with my mother, cooking on the camping stove, and playing with my father on the beach. At night, my brothers and I told ghost stories in our tent with only torches to give us light, long after we were supposed to go to bed. It was the first time I'd ever been camping and I loved it. We go back to that same place every year on my birthday – my parents, my two brothers and I ... it's a sort of tradition now.

UNIT 8 Recording 1

I = interviewer   K = Karen   M = Marta   S = Sam

I: Welcome back, folks. Today we're celebrating Human Achievement Day, where we take a look at great things that the people around us have done in their lives. Today, in particular, we're celebrating people in our lives that have experienced challenges and didn't give up. Those people that keep trying until they're successful. The people that help us and make us want to be better. Today, we're going to hear from you, and hear your stories about the people who are important to you.
First up we have Karen. Karen. Hi! Where are you from and what's your story?

K: Hi! I'm from London and I'm calling to tell you about my grandfather.

I: Great! Go on ...

K: Well, my grandfather was a person who loved adventure, just like me! He travelled all over the world and even climbed the highest mountain in the world, Mount Everest ... twice! Once, when climbing a mountain in France, he and his friend were caught in a snow storm. His friend was injured and couldn't walk but, luckily, my grandfather helped him get back down the mountain to safety. It took him two days, but he didn't give up ... and ... in the end ... he saved his friend's life!

I: Wow! What a great story and what a hero! Thanks, Karen! Next, we have Marta. Marta, where are you from and what's your story?

M: Hi there. I'm from Dublin and I want to tell you about my friend's achievements ... and mine, I suppose.

I: Hm, yes.

M: Well, sadly ... I was in a car accident two years ago and was badly injured. I couldn't walk and I had to stay in hospital for over six months. I was really sad and very worried. Luckily, my friend Laura visited me every day, even though she had a busy job and children. She helped me to get better and even helped me to walk again. Now, thankfully, I'm back to normal and I'm even going to run a marathon next week! All thanks to Laura! In fact, we're going to do the run together!

I: That's great, Marta! Well done! OK, finally we have ... Sam. Sam, hello?

S: Hi! I wanted to talk about my mum. She's great and she's achieved so much.

I: Aw. Go on.

S: Well, I mean, she does everything for me. I still live at home, you see. She does my washing, makes my bed, cooks my dinner and I'm allowed to watch anything I want on TV. My friends tell me I need to move out, I'm 40 next week, but I think they're wrong! Living at home is great!

I: Er ... right ... thanks, Sam. So that's all we have time for today ...

UNIT 9 Recording 1

Pa = Pat   Pe = Pearl   S = Shop assistant   C = Customer
W = Woman   M = Man   TG = Tour guide

Conversation 1

Pa: So where shall we put this? How about the living room?

Pe: Mm, I'm not sure. We already have a lot of pictures in there. What about the bedroom?

Pa: The bedroom might be a good place for it ... Hmm, it's a lovely painting, but I'm not sure about the colours for the bedroom. I don't think it would go with our red wall.

Pe: That's true. I know ... the office, we don't have much in there and we can hang it over our desk.

Pa: Maybe, but I never use the office and I want our guests to see it. There's a story behind the painting, so it would be a shame if no one ever saw it.

Pe: Well I don't know where else to suggest. We need to find somewhere to put it. The toilet?

Pa: That will look silly, Pearl ... I know! The hall. It can go on the wall in the entrance so it's the first thing we see when we come in.

Pe: Great idea. Let's do that.

Conversation 2

S: How can I help, sir?

C: Well, I bought this picture and frame last week in your shop, but I can see a mark on the canvas. I'd like a refund.

S: Could I have a look, sir?

C: Of course. You can see in the corner of the painting, there's a mark.

S: I'm afraid that mark wasn't there when you bought it, sir. We check all paintings before we take payment.

C: Well, the young girl who served me didn't and it was only when I got home that I realised.

S: Well, do you have your receipt?

C: Of course not, it was a tiny piece of paper. I threw it away.

S: I'm very sorry about that, but unfortunately, I can't do anything about it.

C: That's ridiculous. Can I see the manager, please? I'd like to make a complaint.

Conversation 3

W: OK, so we have two hours, what do you think we should do? I fancy some culture.

M: Well, there's an exhibition of photography in the town hall. It's about the oldest tribe in the Amazon. It looks fascinating.

W: Oh, I think I've been to that. It was excellent.

M: Well, if you don't want to go, there's another one with weird sculptures.

W: Sculptures aren't my thing, I find them pretty boring. Let's go to the one on photography. It was so good that I don't mind going back.

Conversation 4

TG: So, here we have one of the artist's last pieces before he died. You can see it's made from stone. It's likely that the two figures we can see are the artist and his life partner, who died in a tragic accident. It's possible that this was the artist's tribute to his partner. You can see that it's difficult to see whose legs and arms are whose and I think this was the sculptor's intention. It seems to me he wanted to show how close the couple were; people say they were inseparable!

UNIT 10 Recording 1

NR = News reporter   M = Mayor   W1 = Woman 1   M1 = Man 1
W2 = Woman   M2 = Man 2

NR: Harrow council has announced plans to convert an old hotel car park into a *park and ride*. The council promises that the new bus service into the town centre will reduce traffic and air pollution. Some people say that the car park will open as a *park and ride* early next year. The local council have said that there will be a frequent bus service every 20 minutes, and they have also promised to offer all-day parking for only two pounds. The mayor spoke to one of our reporters in Harrow.

M: The idea is that people can leave their car and take a direct bus into town rather than drive into the centre. We hope this will encourage people not to drive in the town centre. We have a huge problem with congestion and it is now a top priority. Last year, we considered banning all cars in the town centre, but we had too many people complaining, so we believe this new service is the next best thing.

NR: But what do the people of Harrow think? Let's hear what the locals have to say.

W1: I think it's a great idea. I actually live near the new *park and ride*. In the morning, I can easily spend about half an hour looking for a car parking space in the town centre, so this is wonderful news.

M1: Parking in the town centre is just too expensive. They've said that the bus fare will be one pound and only two pounds for all-day parking – only three pounds for the day! Compared to what I pay now on parking and petrol, this will make a big difference to the community. I'm thrilled!

W2: People drive too fast for me these days. I've been driving for 40 years, but I get more nervous now with the number of cars on the road and especially in the centre. To be honest, I don't feel safe anymore. This new *park and ride* is perfect for me because I will feel much more relaxed taking a bus into town. In fact, I'll probably go in more often!

M2: For people like me, who live in villages outside the town, this is amazing news. It will also help reduce pollution. I'm for anything that will help the environment.

NR: The council has also announced the possible building of park and share car parks where people can meet at a pub, hotel or shop. This system, where one of the drivers leaves their car and continues their journey in another car, has been successful in cities such as Manchester and Belfast. The mayor says that it is still being discussed and nothing is confirmed.

M: We haven't made any decisions about this service. There are many things to consider, for example public security, but it is definitely a possibility for the future. We are always working to improve our community and our first priority is always the safety and happiness of the residents.

ANSWER KEY

1A

1
1 do 2 taking 3 run 4 Getting 5 part 6 as 7 course
8 studying

2
1 Incorrect. My sister is doing a course **in** economics.
2 Correct.
3 Incorrect. I have a degree **in** English and French.
4 Correct.
5 Incorrect. I'm training **as** a tour guide with a local company.
6 Correct.
7 Correct.
8 Incorrect. I work **part-time** in my local supermarket at the
weekends.

3
1 studying 2 pass 3 part 4 in 5 as 6 run/have

4
1 **A:** do, do   **B:** 'm/am
2 **A:** wake   **B:** don't get
3 **A:** has/'s got   **B:** 'm/am
4 **A:** is taking   **B:** want
5 **A:** 'm/am reading   **B:** think
6 **A:** does go   **B:** goes
7 **A:** is/'s going   **B:** am/'m training
8 **A:** are/'re leaving **B:** am/'m coming

5
1 I love my life here. I ✗ living in the centre and working full-time
in an office. It's great! (am/'m)
2 Why ✗ you studying English? (are)
3 They ✗ taking a course in creative writing. It sounds really
interesting. (are/'re)
4 I never see Sara these days. She ✗ studying for a qualification
in marketing and she is working really hard. (is/'s)
5 What ✗ they looking at? (are)
6 Don't use your phone! You ✗ driving! (are/'re)
7 Sorry, but we can't go to the party. We are really busy this month
as we ✗ working on an important project. (are/'re)
8 He ✗ not speaking to her at the moment. They had an argument.
(is/'s)

1B

1
1 reliable 2 caring 3 honest, open 4 patient, sensitive
5 lazy 6 shy, confident 7 ambitious, hard-working
8 organised 9 creative

2
Across
2 hard-working 4 caring 5 ambitious 6 reliable
Down
1 shy 3 organised 4 calm 7 creative

3
1 are/'re 2 am/'m 3 going 4 are 5 to 6 are

4a
1 What is she going to do after university?
2 When are we seeing Tim this week?
3 What are you going to do when you leave school?
4 What course are you starting on Tuesday?
5 How long are they staying next weekend?
6 What is David going to do in the future?

b
1 f 2 e 3 d 4 c 5 a 6 b

1C

1
1 going down 2 improve 3 harder 4 falling
5 decreasing 6 rising

2
1 rising 2 improves 3 falling 4 getting harder
5 getting easier 6 increased 7 go down 8 decrease

3
1 will 2 will 3 help 4 increase 5 use 6 will
7 have 8 replace

4
1 will fall 2 won't go 3 will be 4 will pass 5 will have
6 will rise 7 won't replace 8 Will, get worse

5
1 will come to the party
2 'll/will be angry with
3 won't stay here
4 won't carry money
5 'll/will arrive late
6 'll/will go on holiday

1D

1
1 a 2 b 3 b 4 a 5 b 6 b

2
1 sure 2 not 3 sounds 4 watching 5 for 6 on

3
1 sounds really interesting
2 taking up a hobby
3 not try running
4 on doing sport
5 here's another idea
6 I think
7 a brilliant idea
8 you to forget

Listening

1
1 c

2
1 Not everyone 2 isn't very 3 useful 4 bad
5 in the summer 6 see 7 negative 8 would

3a/b
1 F 2 T 3 T 4 F 5 F 6 T

Reading

1
b

2
1 Social interaction: making small talk and finding things in common with a complete stranger.
2 Ask easy questions at first and don't be afraid to ask personal questions.
3 It makes conversation easier because you have a lot of things to say to each other.
4 Because they might notice and think you're insincere.
5 Words and body language.
6 It can make people feel colder.

3
1 questions   2 interesting   3 talk   4 interested
5 you are cold

4
1 a piece of advice   2 similar   3 good
4 receives guests in their home 5 dishonest

Writing

1
1 senior accountant
2 He has all the necessary skills. / He's managing people in his current job.

2
a M   b B   c E   d B   e M   f E   g E   h M   i B   j E

UNIT 2

2A

1
1 annoyed   2 embarrassed   3 frightened   4 relaxed
5 disappointed   6 worried

2
1 annoying   2 relaxing   3 embarrassed   4 excited
5 frightening   6 surprising   7 tired   8 disappointing
9 worrying   10 embarrassing

3
1 surprised   2 amazing   3 tired   4 worrying   5 relaxing
6 embarrassed   7 excited   8 frightening

4
1 were you doing   2 was   3 Did you see   4 was having
5 were standing   6 was learning   7 was happening   8 heard

5
1 Someone called when I was giving a class.
2 She met her husband when she was studying English at university.
3 I was waiting for a bus for one hour when three came at once!
4 He was travelling when he met an old friend.
5 My niece called when I was watching TV.
6 I was walking to the station when I realised I didn't have my phone.

2B

1
1 reminds   2 think   3 makes   4 of   5 forget   6 memories

2
1 The smell of newly cut grass makes me think of summer.
2 The taste of paella reminds me of holidays in Spain.
3 The sound of birds singing makes me (feel) happy.
4 I'll never forget the day the Berlin Wall came down.
5 I have happy memories of my school days.
6 I'll always remember the day my sister got married.
7 Walking down this road reminds me of when I was young.
8 I'll never forget arriving in Rome.

3
1 I didn't **use** to go camping as a child.
2 I used to **meet** my friends every Saturday.
3 She **didn't use** to like her job, but she does now.
4 He didn't use **to** get good marks at school.
5 I **used** to love the smell of roast chicken, but I can't stand it now!
6 Did you **use** to play sports when you were at school?
7 We used to **smoke**, but we quit a couple of years ago.
8 We **used** to go on holidays to France every summer.

4
1 Mark used to be single, but now he's married.
2 Mark used to wear jeans a lot, but now he wears a suit to work.
3 Mark used to go to school, but now he works in an office.
4 Mark used to do a lot of exercise, but now he doesn't do any exercise.
5 Mark didn't use to cook, but now he loves cooking.
6 Mark used to ride a bicycle, but now he drives a car.
7 Mark used to live with his parents, but now he lives in an apartment.
8 Mark didn't use to travel, but now he goes on holiday twice a year.

2C

1a
1 e   2 a   3 f   4 b   5 d   6 c   7 g   8 h

b

Positive adjectives	Negative adjectives
lively cheerful peaceful	dull homesick anxious stressful unpleasant

2
1 nervous   2 unpleasant   3 homesick   4 optimistic
5 extraordinary   6 strange   7 dull   8 enjoyable   9 cheerful
10 lively

3
1 too tough   2 such   3 so   4 so   5 too   6 enough time
7 exciting enough   8 so

4
1 b   2 c   3 a   4 e   5 d   6 h   7 f   8 g

2D

1
1 What   2 That's   3 Oh no   4 Uh huh

2
1 a   2 b   3 c   4 c   5 a   6 b   7 a   8 a   9 b

Listening

1
1 Claudia (C)   2 Holly (H)   3 David (D)

2
David – smell   Holly – smell   Claudia – sound

3
1 cows 2 safe 3 A smell 4 1988 5 didn't miss
6 smell 7 bookshop 8 first 9 song

Reading

1a
1 nine 2 100,000,000 3 7

2
1 T 2 T 3 F 4 F 5 F

3
1 to remember
2 near the centre of the brain
3 in our long-term memory
4 because the brain makes small changes to memories
5 to keep it active
6 do exercise, sleep at least seven hours a night,
  develop new skills

Writing

1
A Independence
B Make international friends
C Get a better job!
D Learn a language

2
1 topic 2 examples

3
If you take a year out and go somewhere on your own, you quickly learn how to look after yourself.
Travelling around the world or volunteering abroad will mean that you meet new people from different places.
'How can a gap year improve my CV?' you might ask.
A gap year normally means going abroad and learning a language.

UNIT 3

1
1 experiencing 2 perform 3 take up 4 exploring
5 applied 6 going on

2
1 raise 2 explore 3 in 4 applied 5 perform
6 experience 7 go 8 up

3
1 saw 2 have not/haven't gone 3 lived 4 lived
5 Did try 6 Have ever seen 7 have/'ve already eaten
8 has/'s just left 9 have not/haven't done 10 was

4
1 Have you ever been to Dublin?
2 Grace has always wanted to explore the Himalayas.
3 I've been to Berlin several times.
4 Have you seen the new Batman film yet?
5 They haven't been to visit yet.
6 I've never lived abroad.
7 Luca has already raised £10,000 for charity.
8 Has she ever performed in a play?

5
1 for 2 since 3 for 4 for 5 since 6 for

1
1 meet up with 2 hang out 3 catch up on 4 lose touch with
5 got to know 6 get on well

2
1 a 2 b 3 b 4 a 5 c 6 a 7 b 8 b

3
1 I've been working for three hours.
2 I've been sleeping all day.
3 We've lost touch with each other.
4 I haven't seen Ania since June.
5 I've been staying with my friend, so I haven't had time to look at my emails.
6 We've been going to Ireland for our holidays for many years.
7 I've been spending less time at work recently. Before, I was often there until midnight!
8 I haven't seen John this morning.

4
1 What **have** you been doing since I last saw you?
2 This isn't the first time we have **lost** touch.
3 Nazir **has** been spending a lot of time with his friends recently.
4 They have just finished studying for their exams.
5 She **has** performed on stage since she was very young and now she is a professional dancer.
6 I have **done** several courses in art this year.
7 We **have stayed** in touch since he left.
8 I've **been** catching up with friends recently.

1
1 skyline 2 traffic jams 3 landmark 4 cycle lanes
5 outdoor café 6 suburb

2
1 skyline 2 traffic jams 3 cycle lanes 4 cycle lanes
5 traffic jam 6 skylines

3a/b
1 ~~the~~ People 2 ~~a~~ the phone 3 as a teacher
4 The Paris (skyline) 5 The money 6 for ~~the~~ work

4
1 a 2 the 3 the 4 no article 5 a 6 the 7 no article
8 no article 9 a 10 no article 11 the

1
a 1 b 4 c 2 d 5 e 6 f 3

2
1 Sure, walk along this street and take the first road on your left.
2 It's opposite the park.
3 What's the quickest way to Glen Street?
4 How do I get there?
5 Go straight on and the swimming pool is on your left.
6 It's next to a big supermarket.
7 Yes, it's across from the theatre. 8 It's about 15 minutes' walk.

Listening

1
a 2 b 3 c 1 d not mentioned

2

1 20
2 her childhood friends
3 once
4 by phone and by letter
5 He writes occasional letters to friends and uses social media.
6 Her father was in the Air Force.
7 a couple
8 Because your life changes and you may not have things in common any more.

3a/b

a 3 b 1 c 2 d 2 e 1 f 3

Reading

1

b

2

1 quickest, most comfortable
2 So you can write down all your new finds and tell your family and colleagues.
3 You can watch the skyline at sunset, or stop and admire the buildings.
4 We can go a year without seeing our close friends.
5 To do something different to break from routine. You may find a new interest or hobby.
6 Don't take photos and enjoy the moment.

3

1 bus/tour 2 sunset 3 (old) friends 4 different 5 camera

4

1 on your doorstep 2 spot 3 away 4 catching up
5 snapping

Writing

1

1 Shopping and coffee
2 Museums and art galleries
3 Parks
4 Eating and drinking

2

tourists

3

1 C 2 S 3 S 4 C 5 C 6 S

UNIT 4

1

1 inactive 2 easy-going 3 unhealthy 4 sociable
5 stressful 6 energetic 7 healthy 8 sensible

2

1 busy 2 sociable 3 stressful 4 sensible 5 healthy
6 energetic 7 simple

3

1 more stressful 2 slower 3 healthier 4 better
5 more regularly 6 more interested 7 worse 8 better
9 more fattening 10 less active

4

1 It's healthier to cook your own food than eat out.
2 Health is more important than work.
3 Driving a car is worse for the environment than riding a bike.
4 I think working with other people is less boring than working alone.
5 Young people do exercise more regularly than before.
6 I don't mind earning less money if I'm happy.
7 There are fewer people buying houses today than in previous generations.
8 Life in the country is not as stressful as life in the city.

5

1 Snowboarding is more dangerous than skiing.
2 Traffic and pollution in the past wasn't as bad as it is now.
3 There aren't as many people living in villages.
4 Kat could swim better than Sue.
5 Other services are generally not as good as ours.

1

1 Environmentally friendly 2 service 3 Well-designed
4 quality 5 Easy to use 6 Good value 7 reliable

2

1 poor quality 2 environmentally friendly 3 poorly designed
4 high quality 5 excellent service 6 reliable 7 easy to use
8 good value 9 well designed

3

1 nicest 2 worst 3 best 4 friendliest 5 most important
6 least important 7 funniest 8 most popular

4

1 This is **the** easiest route to the city centre.
2 This must be the **loudest** washing machine I've ever had!
3 This restaurant is **the** best in town – everyone knows it!
4 Why did you buy the **cheapest** one?
5 The **best** phones come with good cameras.
6 It's simply the most **reliable**.
7 This is the **worst** meal I've ever had.
8 I think it's the **best** value.

1

1 romantic comedy 2 documentary 3 horror 4 action
5 fantasy 6 animation

2

Across
2 comedy 3 science 6 documentary
Down
1 romantic 4 fantasy 5 horror 6 drama 7 musical

3

1 who 2 where 3 who 4 whose 5 which 6 who
7 which/that 8 where 9 who 10 that

4

1 The film **which/that** cost the most to make was *Spaceplanes*.
2 He's an actor **who** has appeared in many films.
3 It's a moving film **which** tells the story of a young boy growing up in India.
4 I think it's a film **which** will be popular with all ages.
5 She plays a woman **whose** husband is a criminal.
6 It's the famous scene **when** Harry meets Sally.
7 The film is set in a city **where** there are many problems.
8 I like actors **who** are believable.

4D

1
1 him 2 amazing 3 found 4 guess 5 ages 6 best
7 disappointed 8 really

2
1 What 2 kind 3 honest 4 found 5 really 6 ages

3
1 d 2 a 3 e 4 b 5 f 6 c

Listening

1
1 e 2 b 3 a 4 d 5 c

2
1 listen to music 2 at work 3 stressful (and noisy)
4 social media 5 goes to the countryside/goes out of the city
6 walking 7 email 8 organise his life 9 on social media
10 it's reliable 11 they solved her problem quickly
12 presents (for other people) 13 two hours a day
14 takes a book 15 *The Star Man*

Reading

1
1 b 2 a 3 e 4 c 5 d

2
1 F 2 T 3 T 4 F 5 T

3
a 4,5 b 5 c 4 d 3 e 1 f 3 g 5 h 2

Writing

1a
1 A 2 D 3 B 4 C 5 E

b
1 but, however, although 2 in addition 3 because
4 as a result of, so

2
1 because 2 so 3 As a result 4 but 5 However
6 In addition

UNIT 5

5A

1
1 old-fashioned 2 Matching 3 loose 4 casual

2
1 smart 2 got on 3 old-fashioned 4 matching 5 tight
6 fashionable

3
1 b 2 d 3 a 4 c 5 e

4
1 b 2 c 3 c 4 a 5 b 6 a 7 a 8 c

5
1 They **may be** our friends, Jim and Rita, but I can't really see from here.
2 Lisandros seems **to be** very confident about the interview tomorrow, but I know he's nervous.
3 I don't believe it – she **can't be** 50! She looks so young!
4 We **might not** be able to come tomorrow.
5 People **must know** about it. It's in all of the newspapers!
6 She **could** be from France but I'm not sure. She speaks English so well that it's impossible to know!

5B

1
1 d 2 e 3 b 4 c 5 a

2
1 Detached 2 patio 3 air conditioning 4 central heating
5 studio 6 block of flats 7 ceilings 8 floors 9 balcony

3
1 D 2 B 3 E 4 C 5 A

4
1 live 2 don't need 3 have 4 will build 5 come
6 won't be 7 are 8 will be 9 get 10 take

5C

1
1 c 2 d 3 e 4 b 5 a

2
1 spicy 2 cooked 3 bitter 4 grilled 5 sweet 6 roast
7 fried 8 bitter

3
1 savoury 2 homemade 3 tasty 4 grilled 5 fried
6 sweet 7 bitter 8 spicy

4
1 b 2 b 3 b 4 a 5 b 6 a 7 b 8 b

5
1 much 2 bit 3 any 4 enough 5 few
6 much 7 much 8 lots

5D

1
1 First 2 Then 3 Next 4 Finally 5 That's

2
a 6 b 3 c 1 d 4 e 2 f 5

3
1 could you tell me
2 First of all
3 OK, I've got that
4 How long does that take
5 OK, go on
6 Is there anything else
7 No, that's it

Listening

1
a 3 b 1 c 2

2
a 2 b 1 c 3

3a

1 They're going to have uniforms.
2 Because he won't have to spend so much time choosing what to wear.
3 Because she feels her clothes show her personality. / She'll feel like a robot.
4 Tell the boss what she thinks.

b

1 F 2 F 3 T 4 T

c

a 2 b 3 c 1 d 4 e 6 f 5

Reading

1
b

2

1 Tea/chai.
2 India.
3 To have room for lunch.
4 A strong cup of espresso with hot milk.
5 Seaweed.
6 It is fried in butter.
7 Toast and a green salad.
8 Because of the importance of routine and habit, tradition and custom.

3

1 traditional 2 varied 3 room 4 ingredient 5 consists of
6 remain

Writing

1a

1 for ages 2 awesome 3 So 4 get together 5 Anyway
6 doing anything 7 fancy

b

1 Do you fancy it 2 let me know 3 have you been in touch
4 awesome 5 Anyway 6 ages 7 Speak soon

2

1 T 2 T 3 T 4 F 5 T

UNIT 6

1

1 Turn up 2 Unload 3 Load 4 Fill 5 Empty 6 Turn down
7 Switch on 8 Load

2

1 switch off 2 filling 3 Loading 4 charge 5 Turning down
6 switching on 7 switch on 8 switch it off

3

1 b 2 h 3 e 4 c 5 a 6 f 7 d 8 g

4

1 If they knew, they would tell me.
2 If I had more free time, I would learn Japanese.
3 If we walked more, we would be healthier.
4 If we didn't have mobile phones, we would talk more.
5 If he didn't have a car, he wouldn't get to work on time.

5

1 What would change if we didn't have mobile phones?
2 What would happen if the internet went down?
3 If there were fewer cars on the roads, would it be better for the environment?
4 What would I do if I didn't live in the city centre?

6

a Of course. If people used more public transport, there would be less pollution.
b If we didn't spend so much time on our phones, we would have better conversations with our friends and family.
c We would call Dad and get it reconnected!
d I don't know! If you lived in the countryside, I'm sure you wouldn't like it.

7

1 b 2 c 3 a 4 d

6b

1

1 d 2 f 3 a 4 b 5 c 6 e

2

1 rude 2 the law 3 illegal 4 dishonest 5 fair

3

1 b 2 b 3 a 4 a 5 b 6 a 7 a 8 b

4

1 What do you think I should do? 2 If I were you
3 I think you should 4 I ought to 5 You shouldn't
6 So what should

6c

1

1 a 2 b 3 h 4 e 5 a 6 f 7 c 8 g

2

1 throw away 2 reduce 3 recycle 4 save 5 kill
6 destroy 7 reuse 8 protect

3

1 do 2 don't 3 aren't 4 hasn't 5 wouldn't 6 it 7 is
8 they 9 will 10 isn't 11 don't we 12 you

4

1 do you 2 can't we 3 doesn't it 4 don't we 5 is it
6 aren't there 7 can we 8 isn't there

6d

1

1 Would you mind
2 afraid I can't do that
3 sure, no problem
4 It depends
5 If it wouldn't be too much trouble

2

a 2 b 6 c 3 d 7 e 8 f 1 g 4 h 5 i 9 j 11 k 10

Listening

1

a 5 b 1 c 4 d 2 e 3

2

1 F 2 T 3 F 4 T 5 F 6 F 7 T

3
b

74

Reading

1

1 b 2 a 3 c

2

1 She saw some cruel messages on her daughter's phone.
2 When she lost her job.
3 She doesn't want to lend her friend anything else and is worried that she will ask for something.
4 The thrill/excitement.
5 To talk to her friend.

3

1 e 2 d 3 a 4 b 5 c

Writing

1

2 ✓ 5 ✓

2

1 There are different views on this subject
2 Many people think that
3 In addition
4 On the other hand
5 In addition
6 In conclusion
7 However

3

Paragraph A: 3
Paragraph B: 1
Paragraph C: 4
Paragraph D: 2

UNIT 7

1

1 create 2 gain 3 take 4 gain 5 improve
6 change 7 uploading

2

1 design 2 edit 3 prepare 4 improve 5 gain 6 work on
7 improve 8 learn

3

1 Could you 2 Were you able 3 couldn't 4 be able to
5 can't 6 won't be able

4

1 can dance 2 couldn't do 3 able to 4 able to 5 can't find
6 can't 7 wasn't able to/couldn't 8 was able to

1

1 f 2 h 3 g 4 a 5 b 6 d 7 e 8 c

2

1 gone 2 got 3 moved 4 lost 5 find 6 fallen 7 passed
8 win

3

1 When I arrived at the station, the train had left.
2 I'd finished university before I moved to Spain.
3 By the time he turned 20, he'd lost five jobs!
4 After I'd travelled through Europe, I went to Africa.
5 I'd always wanted to be an actress.
6 I didn't know what to do after I'd left school.

4

1 After 2 already 3 By 4 after 5 before 6 by

5

1 Pete **lost** his job last month, so he's looking for a new one.
2 I had just decided to take the new job when my boss ~~had~~ asked me to stay.
3 Before Anya learnt to drive, her dad **had** already bought her a new car.
4 By the time he was 18, Chris **had** already left home.
5 She **had** already won the lottery twice when she won a million euros last month.
6 Kirsten **had** lived in the house for a long time when she decided to sell it.
7 When they got married, they **had** already known each other for ten years.

1

1 backpack 2 jacket 3 boots 4 stove
5 repellent 6 charger

2

1 tent 2–3 (in any order) sunscreen, sunglasses
4 camping stove 5 portable charger 6 insect repellent
7 torch

3

1 torch 2 sunscreen 3 waterproof jacket
4 insect repellent 5 sleeping bag 6 sunglasses
7 portable charger 8 tent

4

1 so 2 for 3 so that 4 so that 5 to 6 to 7 to 8 for

5

1 f 2 c 3 a 4 g 5 b 6 d 7 e 8 h

1

1 Is there anything else I can do for you?
2 Can I help you?
3 Can you tell me what time they start?
4 Do you offer English classes?
5 Can you give me some information about what courses you offer?
6 Could you say that again?
7 Would you mind sending me a brochure?
8 I wonder if you could give me some advice?

2

1 calling to 2 can I 3 Could you 4 got that 5 interested in
6 you mind

Listening

1

1 Sarah A 2 Jude C 3 Georgina B

2

Sarah: The Amazon, South America / Wedding anniversary
Jude: Paris / She loved French culture and food
Georgina: The north of England / For her seventh birthday

3

1 first 2 backpack/walking boots 3 Europe 4 university
5 she's heard it's changed a lot 6 seven 7 ghost stories

Reading

1
Student's own answers.

3
1 He decided to take more time for himself.
2 He takes the time to laugh every day.
3 About five years ago.
4 So that she could meet the demand and continue to make clothes.
5 He needed to do something different.
6 He went to South Africa on a wildlife safari.
7 Because it's been shown to reduce stress and increase levels of happiness.

4
1 joking (to joke) 2 demand 3 to switch off 4 to book
5 solution

Writing

1
1 d 2 e 3 c 4 b 5 a

2
imperatives: come and support us, call Laura, visit
adjectives: passionate, historic, rich, great, perfect

3
1 B 2 B 3 A 4 B 5 B 6 A

UNIT 8

1
1 up 2 in 3 out 4 in 5 away 6 with 7 back 8 down
2
1 down 2 back 3 back 4 away 5 with 6 out
3
1 ✓ 2 N 3 ✓ 4 N 5 ✓ 6 ✓ 7 N
4
1 must 2 need 3 allowed 4 need 5 need 6 need
7 must
5
1 don't have to 2 need to 3 were allowed to 4 had to
5 mustn't

8B

1
1 Thankfully 2 Amazingly 3 Hopefully 4 Obviously
5 strangely 6 Unfortunately 7 Luckily 8 Tragically
2
1 tragically 2 Sadly 3 Amazingly 4 Luckily
5 Unfortunately 6 Hopefully
3
1 e 2 d 3 b 4 f 5 g 6 h 7 c 8 a
4
1 was 2 is being 3 were rescued 4 found 5 was given
6 being

5
1 The hikers were found by the rescue team.
2 New equipment is being tested by experts.
3 A new treatment for back injuries was discovered (by scientists).
4 The games are being held in Moscow.
5 The room wasn't being used when we arrived.
6 The Lake District was made a World Heritage site (by UNESCO) in 2017.

1
1 snow-covered 2 rocky 3 high 4 clear 5 steep 6 sandy
2
1 mountains 2 rivers 3 Mountains 4 forest 5 lake
6 beaches 7 hills 8 rainforest 9 waterfall 10 valley
11 cliff 12 peak
3
1 where 2 when 3 who 4 where 5 which 6 who
7 whose 8 when
4
1 The ancient mountain, which is 2,000 metres high, gives you the best view of the surroundings.
2 The national park, where you can see lots of wildlife, is in the north of England.
3 April is the best time to visit Seville, when it's not too hot.
4 Here you find the most famous lakes whose beauty you'll never forget.
5 The Awa tribe, who are approximately 200 years old, live in the Amazon.

8D

1
1 b 2 a 3 d 4 c
2
1 really 2 had 3 no 4 see 5 never mind
3
a 1 b 6 c 9 d 2 e 3 f 8 g 7 h 4 i 5 j 10

Listening

1
1 F 2 T
2a
1 all over the world 2 two
3 He had an accident on a mountain. 4 two days
b
1 F 2 F 3 F 4 T
c
1 a 2 a 3 b

Reading

1
C, E, A, D, B
2
1 a 2 c 3 b 4 b 5 c 6 b 7 b
3
1 English classes 2 England 3 Main Manor 4 Meals
5 Landwork castle

Writing

1

Positives:
Speaking the language, the food and culture, the people, the weather, surfing.

Negatives:
Missing friends and family, moving country is expensive, companies want somebody who speaks fluent Spanish.

2

Adding ideas:
as well as, also, and, plus, too, besides

Contrasting ideas:
on the one hand/on the other hand, even though, but

3

1 You love the culture and the food.
2 You'll meet new friends as well as learn new skills. /
   As well as making new friends, you'll learn new skills.
3 On the one hand, moving to Spain will be stressful.
   On the other hand, you'd be bored if you stayed here.
4 You might feel lonely even though there will be lots of opportunities to meet people.

UNIT 9

 9A

1
1 save up for   2 look for   3 deal   4 wait for   5 goes
6 goods   7 in cash   8 by credit card   9 keep   10 a refund

2
1 pay for/goods   2 look for/bargains   3 save up for/holiday
4 go/on sale   5 cancel/order   6 keep/receipts
7 wait for/sales   8 get/refund

3
1 b   2 e   3 c   4 d   5 f   6 a

4
1 Jobs have been lost.
2 A lot of goods were bought from local farmers and shops in the past.
3 Purchases are paid for online by a lot of people.
4 Changes must be made by high street shops.
5 Cash will not be used in the future.
6 Packages may soon be delivered by robots.

5
1 Customers cancelled orders due to the wait.
2 A lot of people are using credit cards instead of cash today.
3 The man over there has paid for the drinks.
4 Computers will do everything in the future.
5 Companies may soon develop mobile apps that choose our clothes and food for us.
6 Staff gave customers paper receipts.
7 The detective was following him.
8 Do the work by Friday.

 9B

1
1 huge   2 exhausted   3 disgusting   4 terrified   5 furious
6 thrilled   7 excellent   8 tiny

2
1 small   2 angry   3 happy   4 tired   5 big   6 bad
7 scared   8 good

3

1 We wouldn't have known if he hadn't ~~have~~ told us.
2 If they hadn't ~~have~~ been so exhausted, they would have gone to the party.
3 If Jim had ~~to~~ studied harder at school, he would have passed his exams.
4 Would ~~have~~ things have changed if she had won?
5 The teacher wouldn't have been so furious if you ~~would~~ had done your homework properly.
6 If he hadn't reminded me, ~~if~~ I might have forgotten to call.
7 ~~If~~ I wouldn't have spoken to him if I had known who he was.
8 What would have ~~had~~ happened if he hadn't met your mother?

4

1 If I had known you were in hospital, I would have visited you.
2 If they hadn't been late, they wouldn't have missed the concert.
3 If I hadn't moved to Brazil, I wouldn't have met Charlie.
4 If Tom had studied, he wouldn't have failed his exams.
5 If he hadn't run away, the bear would have killed him.

5

1 If Ben hadn't woken up late, he wouldn't have missed his bus.
2 If he hadn't been late for work, his boss wouldn't have fired him.
3 If he hadn't lost his job, he wouldn't have decided to go to the beach.
4 If he hadn't decided to go to the beach, he wouldn't have met his ex-girlfriend there.
5 If he hadn't met his ex-girlfriend again, they wouldn't have fallen in love again.

 9C

1a
1 original   2 colourful   3 cheerful   4 realistic   5 fascinating
6 powerful   7 creative

b
1 old fashioned/traditional   2 creative/wierd
3 realistic/original   4 colourful/cheerful   5 ugly/awful

2
1 Me neither   2 Me too   3 So have I   4 Nor do I   5 I do too
6 I didn't either   7 Neither have I   8 So are we

3
1 am   2 do   3 neither   4 don't   5 have   6 too   7 did
8 have

 9D

1
1 a   2 c   3 d   4 b   5 f   6 e

2
1 help you   2 I'm afraid   3 seems to be   4 about that
5 Unfortunately I   6 Can I   7 bring me

3
a 1   b 4   c 5   d 2   e 6   f 3   g 7   h 9   i 8   j 10

Listening

1
1 d   2 b   3 c   4 a

2
1 c   2 a   3 c   4 b

3
1 a   2 d   3 d   4 b

Reading

1
1 OY or YO? 2 The first generation in a new country
3 The Sagrada Familia chocolate sculpture 4 Newton
5 The shoes on the Danube Bank

2
1 First generation sculpture 2 Newton
3 The Shoes on the Danube Bank
4 The Sagrada Familia chocolate sculpture 5 OY or YO?

3
1 a 2 b 3 b 4 a 5 a 6 b 7 a 8 a 9 a

Writing

1
a 3 b 1 c 5 d 4 e 2 f 7 g 6

2
1 My granddad's hair is as white as snow.
2 From the plane, the people looked like ants.
3 He's as cold as ice.
4 She was as sweet as a summer's day.

UNIT 10

 10A

1
1 a 2 b 3 c 4 c 5 a 6 b 7 c 8 a

2
1 c 2 e 3 d 4 a 5 g 6 b 7 h 8 f

3
1 Lisa said she had passed her exams
2 The teacher said the best idea was to study hard for tests.
3 They told me they had attended private school.
4 James told us he was revising for his exams so he couldn't go.
5 The mayor said that universities would be free for everybody in the future.
6 Dan and Mark told me the new teacher had really helped them.
7 The students say that they don't want to pay more college fees.
8 The group of teachers said they need more money and more time to plan their lessons.

4
1 He **told me** he wasn't happy.
2 They told us **they** would leave and get new jobs.
3 Correct
4 He said he **didn't like** boarding schools.
5 They said they **had** graduated from university.
6 Correct
7 They told me studying together **would** help them pass their exams.

 10B

1
1 suggested 2 warned 3 promised 4 advised
5 demanded 6 recommended

2
1 avoided 2 persuaded 3 refused 4 considered
5 started 6 warned 7 promised 8 recommended

3
1 a 2 c 3 b 4 b 5 a 6 c 7 c 8 b

4
1 I promise to arrive on time in future.
2 I recommend going on the bus.
3 You'll never persuade me to go ice skating.
4 You should avoid eating oily foods, (they'll make you feel bad).
5 Sorry, but I refuse to go to another one of his stupid meetings.
6 I advise you to travel more.
7 I encouraged her to say something at the meeting.
8 She suggested waiting half an hour before leaving.
9 People start arriving at the office at/after nine. /
People don't start arriving at the office before/until nine.
10 He warned me not to go there at night.

⬥ 10C

1
1 serve customers 2 interview people 3 write reports
4 give presentations 5 do research 6 set up meetings
7 work in a team

2
1 b 2 c 3 d 4 a

3
1 1 John asked Jane how she had passed the test.
2 I asked him if he recommended studying at the weekend.
3 We asked him to give us an example.
4 She wanted to know what I had done in my last job.
5 They asked me what experience I had.
6 She asked me what countries I had been to.
7 They asked me why I wanted the job.
8 He asked me where I would be in five years' time.

4
1 They asked Mike if he had experience in this area.
2 They asked Mike if he enjoyed writing reports.
3 They asked Mike if he had any qualifications.
4 They wanted to know what his greatest skill was.
5 They asked Mike where he was working last year.
6 They asked Mike where he would be in ten years' time.
7 They wanted to know if he liked working in a team.
8 They asked Mike why he wanted to work there.

⬥ 10D

1
1 Interviewer 2 Interviewee 3 Interviewee 4 Interviewer
5 Interviewer 6 Interviewee 7 Interviewer 8 Interviewer

2
1 What made you decide to become a teacher?
2 Can you tell me more about your experience?
3 I think I'd say dedicated, reliable and responsible.
4 As you can see from my CV, I've got excellent IT skills.
5 Why do you want to work for this company?
6 What are your goals for the future?
7 So do you have any questions for me?
8 Could you tell me about your hobbies?
9 I'd be interested to read it!

Listening

1
a 5 b 1 c 2 d 4 e 3

2
1 park and ride 2 20 minutes 3 not to drive 4 car parking space
5 expensive 6 safe 7 pollution 8 hotel/shop

Reading

1

a

2

1 T 2 F 3 T 4 F 5 T 6 T 7 T 8 F

3

1 M 2 M 3 B 4 M 5 B 6 M 7 M 8 B 9 B 10 B

Writing

1

1 the violin 2 Because it's old and not very good.

3 Because he works until nine. 4 In order to get a discount.

2

1 a 2 e 3 d 4 f 5 c 6 d

Pearson Education Limited
KAO TWO
KAO Park
Hockham Way
Harlow
Essex
CM17 9SR
England
and Associated Companies throughout the world.

english.com/roadmap

First published 2019

Sixth impression 2023

ISBN: 978-1-292-22815-0

Set in Soho Gothic Pro

Printed in Great Britain by Ashford Colour Press Ltd.

Photo acknowledgements
*The publisher would like to thank the following for their kind permission to
reproduce their photographs:*

123RF.com: Filipe Frazao 43, georgejmclittle 9, stefbennett 13; **Alamy Stock
Photo:** Ian Dagnall 45, James Cheadle 37, Simon Dack News 54, Wavebreak
Media ltd 6; **Getty Images:** Alberto Bogo 31, Ashley Baxter, girlwithacamera.
co.uk 32, Bruno Vincent 27, Buena Vista Images , DigiPub 32, FatCamera 47, Herianus Herianus / EyeEm 36, Kathy Medcalf Photography 48, Mariusz Kluzniak
21, Westend61 12, Zephyr18 44; **Pearson Education Ltd:** Tudor Photography
25; **Shutterstock.com:** 41, 44, Atstock Productions 23, Critterbiz 53, Dariusz
Jarzabek 29, EmBaSy 25, Ewelina Wachala 29, Gena Melendrez 35, Gorodenkoff
44, JeniFoto 59, Johann Knox 50, Juanamari Gonzalez 51, Kiko Jimenez 57, Larina
Marina 36, Leonard Zhukovsky 56, Leszek Glasner 37, Londowl 45, Martti Kainu-
lainen 10, Melory 40, Mikbiz 61, Nikonaft 43, Rawpixel.com 46, 8, Resul Muslu
19, SJ Travel Photo and Video 34, Song_about_summer 5, Syda Productions 62,
62, Thanaprus.N 43, Torwaistudio 16, Val Thoermer 11, Vixit 49, Vladgrin 14,
Vladyslav Starozhylov 26, Zilu8 25, cobalt88 25, domnitsky 25, eightshot 38,
fizkes 60, 63, icemanphotos 48, lkoimages 50, sirtravelalot 55, solominviktor
20, spirit of america 18, travellight 50.

Cover Images: *Front:* **Getty Images:** Buena Vista Images